RAND

The Origins and Evolution of Family Planning Programs in Developing Countries

Judith R. Seltzer

Supported by the
William and Flora Hewlett Foundation
David and Lucile Packard Foundation
Rockefeller Foundation

POPULATION MATTERS

A RAND Program of Policy-Relevant Research Communication

The research described in this report was supported by the William and Flora Hewlett Foundation, the David and Lucile Packard Foundation, and the Rockefeller Foundation.

Library of Congress Cataloging-in-Publication Data

Seltzer, Judith R., 1948-
   The origins and evolution of family planning programs in developing coutries /
Judith R. Seltzer.
     p. cm.
    "MR-1276."
    Includes bibliographical references.
    ISBN 0-8330-2928-2
    1. Birth control—Developing countries—History. 2. Federal aid to birth
control—Developing countries—History. 3. Birth control—Developing countries—
Management. 4. Population policy—Developing countries. I. Title.

HQ766.5.D44 S45 2002
363.9'6'091724—dc21

                                  2001048313

RAND is a nonprofit institution that helps improve policy and decisionmaking through research and analysis. RAND® is a registered trademark. RAND's publications do not necessarily reflect the opinions or policies of its research sponsors.

Published 2002 by RAND
1700 Main Street, P.O. Box 2138, Santa Monica, CA 90407-2138
1200 South Hayes Street, Arlington, VA 22202-5050
201 North Craig Street, Suite 102, Pittsburgh, PA 15213-1516
RAND URL: http://www.rand.org/
To order RAND documents or to obtain additional information,
contact Distribution Services: Telephone: (310) 451-7002;
Fax: (310) 451-6915; Email: order@rand.org

Family planning programs occupy an unusual place in the public policy arena. They are widespread, judging by their near ubiquity around the globe, and also generally considered an effective public health policy. Yet, family planning programs are persistently controversial. In part because they center on birth control, a sensitive subject that stirs strong views, they have drawn criticism from a wide range of perspectives: religious, political, ideological, and scientific. This report examines the criticisms and controversies that have surrounded family planning. It attempts to place these in historical context and examine how programs have evolved in response to these criticisms and to shifting currents in the policy arena. It also examines the research record to assess the validity of these criticisms. The intent in surveying this historical record is to enable readers to view current debates about family planning in a broader historical context and to provide a stronger grounding in the research evidence associated with some of the claims made by both proponents and critics of family planning.

This research was conducted for *Population Matters*, a RAND project to synthesize and communicate the policy-relevant results of demographic research. Through publications and outreach activities, the project aims to raise awareness and highlight the importance of population policy issues and to provide a scientific basis for public debate over population policy questions. *Population Matters* is part of RAND's Labor and Population Program.

The *Population Matters* project is funded by grants from the William and Flora Hewlett Foundation, the David and Lucile Packard

Foundation, and the Rockefeller Foundation. For further information and access to other *Population Matters* publications, visit www.rand.org/labor/popmatters.

CONTENTS

TABLES

Family planning programs exist in virtually every nation. As of 1998, 179 countries with 99 percent of the world's population had some form of family planning program. Despite their pervasiveness, family planning programs have caused controversy and drawn criticism from a variety of perspectives, primarily for two reasons. First, they deal with a sensitive subject: birth control. Public discussion of the issue was taboo for many years and continues to evoke strong reactions from some quarters. Adding to this sensitivity, the emotionally charged debate over abortion has at times spilled over into the discussion of family planning. Second, concern about the negative effects of rapid population growth and high fertility in the developing world spawned a political advocacy movement that promoted particular public policies, family planning among them. While this movement enjoyed considerable support in both developing and donor nations, it also generated political opposition and raised questions among some social scientists and others.

This report examines the origins and evolution of family planning programs in the context of the major criticisms and controversies surrounding them. It also explores how programs have responded to these criticisms and assesses the validity of these criticisms as reflected in the research literature. Although some of the criticisms are based on ideological perspectives that scientific research does little to illuminate, simply describing these perspectives should be useful.

The research questions include the following:

- What were the guiding rationales of family planning programs in developing countries?

- What have been the main criticisms of family planning programs and were they valid?

- How has research contributed to understanding whether the criticisms were valid?

- How have programs changed in response to criticisms and concerns?

- What can lessons and implications for policy can be drawn from understanding the criticisms and the research on family planning programs?

ORIGINS AND RATIONALES OF FAMILY PLANNING PROGRAMS

In the 1960s, U.S. foundations (such as the Ford and Rockefeller Foundations), international development agencies, and governments in a number of developing nations shared fears about the potential consequences of rapid population growth and high fertility. Surveys showed that a substantial proportion of women in developing countries did not want more children, but were not practicing contraception. The development of two new contraceptive methods—the oral contraceptive pill and the intrauterine device (IUD)—raised hopes that effective, inexpensive contraception could be made widely available to fill this "unmet need."

There was widespread optimism that establishing programs to distribute contraceptives on a large scale would help achieve several policy objectives: reducing population growth and (unwanted) high fertility and thus boosting standards of living; improving women's health and quality of life by helping them avoid unintended pregnancies and abortion; and advancing the rights of couples and women to plan their families. These three distinct but interrelated objectives, or rationales, have furnished the legitimating premise for family planning programs from the beginning.

Demographic Rationale

Reducing high fertility rates and slowing population growth provided the dominant rationale for family planning programs in the 1960s and 1970s. This rationale was based on concerns over the potentially negative effects of rapid population growth and high fertility on living standards and human welfare, economic productivity, natural resources, and the environment in the developing world.

Health Rationale

During the 1980s, a different set of concerns became paramount: the public health consequences of high fertility for mothers and children. High rates of infant, child, and maternal mortality, as well as abortion and its health consequences, were pressing health problems in many developing nations and had also become of greater concern to international development agencies. High maternal mortality was associated with high-risk circumstances that family planning could help to address. These included a high number of pregnancies, births to older and younger women, and pregnancies that were unintended. In addition, closely spaced births were associated with higher rates of infant morbidity and mortality. This rationale extended to issues of equity: Government-sponsored family planning programs could provide poor women with the same access to services that wealthier women already enjoyed through private physicians.

Human Rights Rationale

This rationale became preeminent in the 1990s, in part because of reactions to excesses under the demographic rationale. The human rights rationale rests on the belief that individuals and couples have a fundamental right to control reproductive decisions, including family size and the timing of births. This rationale found its strongest articulation at the International Conference on Population and Development (ICPD), held in Cairo, Egypt, in 1994.

All three rationales have existed from the early days of family planning programs, but they have been given different emphasis over time. All three are relevant today. Despite the increased attention to human rights by many human rights and health advocates and international organizations, most developing country governments continue to emphasize the demographic rationale.

ASSESSING THE MAIN CRITICISMS OF FAMILY PLANNING PROGRAMS

What follows is a capsule portrait of the main criticisms of family planning programs and an assessment of how valid the criticisms were based on the most current research evidence.

Criticisms of Demographic Objectives

The demographic objectives of family planning programs were based on three assumptions: (1) Rapid population growth impedes economic development, and lower rates of population growth and lower fertility will lead to improved living standards and human welfare. (2) Couples in developing countries want fewer children and are interested in regulating their fertility. (3) Making contraception widely available is an effective way to meet couples' need for fertility regulation and to help lower fertility levels. Most recently, population declines in several countries have raised questions about whether rapid population growth and high fertility continue to pose problems.

Economic Development. Concerns about the impact of rapid population growth assumed that such growth would serve as a brake on economic development and that efforts to improve living standards in developing countries would be a threat to food supplies, natural resources, and the environment. The debate over the link between rapid population growth and economic development continued for years because the research was inadequate to address the question. Research evidence from the 1990s has shown that this criticism was largely unfounded.[1] Slowing population growth and reducing high fertility can matter a great deal for economic growth in developing countries, but appropriate economic policies must be in place to realize the economic benefits of moderating fertility. This research supports assumptions made in the early years of family planning about the relationship between population growth and development.

---

[1] A new report from *Population Matters* describes this research in greater depth (Bloom, Canning, and Sevilla, forthcoming).

Effectiveness of Family Planning Programs. The efficacy of family planning programs to provide contraceptive services and to contribute to lower fertility, and ultimately to lower population growth, was another key part of the debate over demographic objectives. Those questioning the appropriate role and efficacy of programs included not only social scientists, but also feminists and women's rights advocates. The research evidence gathered over many years has found family planning programs to be an effective public policy in many developing countries. The research has shown that family planning programs have helped increase the prevalence of contraception, and this contributed substantially to reduced fertility rates. While these programs have been effective independent of improvements in social and economic development, the level of development in a given setting has also been important for reducing fertility.

The effectiveness of family planning programs was premised on the assumption that couples in developing countries wanted fewer children, and that to achieve smaller families, they would practice contraception. The evidence supporting this assumption has come from surveys that have been carried out since the 1960s. The surveys of women and couples provided information about their attitudes regarding desired family size, whether they wanted to have additional children and if so when, and contraception. Over more than 35 years, these surveys have shown that a large proportion of couples had favorable attitudes toward contraception and that many couples wanted no more children. The surveys also showed that among those not wanting more children, many were not practicing contraception. The discrepancy between women's stated preferences for children (both the number and the timing) and their actual contraceptive use is referred to as the "unmet need" for family planning. Reducing or filling this unmet need has been an objective of family planning programs for many years.

Future Population Growth or Implosion? Some recent commentators on public policy have sounded an alarm about a coming population implosion, implying that population growth is no longer an important policy concern and therefore that the importance of family planning as a public policy has diminished considerably. However, this discussion has tended to focus selectively on Western Europe and a few other highly developed nations, such as Japan. While substantial declines in fertility have taken place in many of these nations in the past half-century, global population growth is projected to continue well into the 22nd century. There remain great variations among regions and countries in levels of population growth and fertility. The world as a whole and many nations, especially in the developing world, will continue to grow. At the same time, many countries are slowly diminishing in population size, causing their populations to age. Adjusting to an aging population is one of the demographic challenges facing the more developed countries. For most of the world's nations, however, the major demographic challenge over the next several decades will continue to be reducing mortality and fertility through a combination of economic growth and social sector programs, including those in education and health.

Health Objectives

The health objectives of family planning programs have prompted five main concerns and controversies. First, women's health advocates and feminists have criticized the prominent role of contraceptive technology and also raised concerns about contraceptive safety. The second issue is whether there were indeed health benefits associated with regulating fertility. The third—and one of the more controversial aspects—is the relationship between abortion and contraceptive use. Fourth, women's health advocates and feminists also raised concerns over the quality of care in family planning programs. The final issue, again voiced by women's health advocates and feminists, is the broader context of reproductive health for family planning services.

Narrow Focus on Contraceptive Technology. Critics of the role of contraceptive technology questioned whether programs would be the technological fix that proponents assumed. Many health advocates among them also raised concerns about the safety of various contraceptive methods for women's health and about scientists' approach to the development of new contraceptives. Many of these concerns were valid. As a result, women's health advocates have contributed to the evolution of programs by ensuring more attention to contraceptive safety issues and also by urging more emphasis on the broader context of women's lives, especially the social and cultural influences that can affect women's ability to take advantage of modern contraception. These health advocates have also enhanced consideration of women's perspectives as contraceptive development and research programs establish their research priorities.

Health Benefits of Family Planning. The health benefits of family planning were increasingly documented thanks to research studies published in the 1980s. The research confirmed that family planning—women's use of safe and effective contraception—helps to reduce maternal mortality by reducing the number of births and high-risk pregnancies. Research also showed that family planning had the potential to improve child health and survival by reducing the number of births associated with higher risks (births that were closely spaced, births to older women, and higher-order births). The documented health benefits of family planning also became an important consideration in the adoption of national population policies, especially in African countries.

Abortion. In recent years, the question of whether family planning programs advocate or promote abortion has figured prominently in the U.S. policy debate over public funding for family planning programs overseas. Since 1974, U.S. law has prohibited the use of American foreign aid funds to support abortion services. However, a growing body of research conducted in many areas, including Bangladesh and the former Soviet Union, has shown that the presence of quality family planning services can reduce abortion. It is also increasingly recognized that some women will choose to end unintended pregnancies through abortion, whether legal or illegal in their countries. A critical challenge for family planning and reproductive health programs is to ensure adequate access to postabortion care, which includes contraception counseling and services, to prevent future abortions.

Quality of Care Provided by Family Planning Programs. For more than a decade, there has been increased interest in the quality of care provided by family planning programs. Health care advocates, feminists, and others pointed to evidence—such as levels of discontinuation of contraceptive use and the unmet need for contraception—that implies that clients' needs and quality of care were not receiving sufficient attention. These concerns helped stimulate considerable research aimed at improving the quality of family planning services. Studies that assess the effects of improved quality have shown initial, promising results. Efforts to measure and improve the quality of care

are ongoing issues for health services in countries around the world and for the international donor community.

Reproductive Health Context. A major change occurred in the 1990s, marked by the 1994 ICPD, in the framework for population policy and programs and also in emphasis of family planning programs. Women's health advocates and feminists formed the vanguard of those seeking to shift these policies' and programs' emphasis from demographic objectives to human rights. Particular attention was given to women's right to reproductive autonomy and empowering women to enable them to secure this right. Furthermore, the broader context of reproductive health, of which family planning is one of several basic reproductive health services, has been widely endorsed by nations around the world and international donor organizations. Research has also been supported in response to the endorsement of reproductive health. The broader agenda for reproductive health requires additional resources, which were forthcoming in the first several years after ICPD. However, donor support has fallen short of the goals set in 1994. Without additional funding, existing resources are being spread more broadly, which will likely dilute the potential impact of reproductive health initiatives, including family planning services.

Human Rights

Human rights advocates have contended that the emphasis on demographic goals and targets of some government programs in developing countries may interfere with women's rights to autonomy in decisions about childbearing and contraception. These criticisms have been frequently validated by research. Goal- or target-oriented programs in several nations—notably China, India, and Indonesia—have exhibited varying degrees of coercion. These criticisms have resulted in a number of policy and program changes and have heightened the sensitivity of international donor organizations to these issues. At the same time, many government-sponsored family planning programs continue to emphasize macro-level population goals along with an increased attention to individual rights and concerns. Other human rights issues have also been raised over the years as family planning programs were established and evolved; these issues include fears of Western cultural intrusion and possible religious objections.

Cultural Intrusiveness. Critics have raised concerns about whether family planning programs represent a form of cultural intrusion into the affairs of developing countries. Research has contributed to a clearer understanding of this issue. Surveys of women in developing countries have shown both widespread desire to regulate fertility and an acceptance of family planning in nearly all countries. Cultural issues have figured most prominently in program implementation and service delivery. Many programs have adapted services to fit cultural contexts, such as providing door-to-door delivery in more traditional Islamic countries where women are discouraged from appearing in certain public settings. Community participation in program development has been key in addressing cultural concerns.

Religious Concerns. Concerns about respecting religious teachings in particular localities have been a long-standing consideration for many family planning programs. Perhaps the strongest opposition comes from the Catholic Church, which condemned artificial contraception in 1930. The Church views contraception as immoral because it may promote marital infidelity. However, the teachings and beliefs of most religious traditions are diverse and complex, making it difficult to generalize about the impact of religious responses. Studies have shown that religious concerns over family planning programs vary widely in developing countries, and that such programs are not incompatible with the beliefs of many. Thus it is not surprising that the majority of couples from Catholic, Islamic, and Buddhist countries uses contraception. One important observation from the research is that involving religious leaders in policy development has improved acceptance and understanding of family planning programs and in turn helped programs adapt to local religious contexts.

LESSONS FOR FUTURE POLICIES

What lessons emerge from reviewing the criticisms and controversies surrounding family planning?

- A central lesson is the value of research. Research continues to be vital in understanding where and why programs have been most effective and where the need for them remains greatest.

- Despite enormous progress in meeting global demand for contraception and related family planning services in the past 35 years, significant challenges remain for satisfying unmet need for contraception in the developing world. About one billion adolescents—the most in history—will soon be entering their years of sexual activity and childbearing. They will be among the growing numbers of women and couples seeking services and with unmet needs. Satisfying their needs will add considerably to the challenges of service delivery in the future.

- Adapting the health care rationale to current global conditions will require revisiting existing organizational and financing arrangements. New combinations of reproductive health services, particularly those that address sexually transmitted diseases and HIV/AIDS, will require reconfiguring services as well as new expertise, training, and financial resources.

- Government and donor organizations should continue to involve women's groups and health advocates in policymaking. Criticisms from these groups have contributed greatly to improvements in program design and implementation.

ACKNOWLEDGMENTS

The author would like to acknowledge those individuals who have provided useful comments and guidance in the course of this report's preparation. The three "formal" reviewers, Albert Hermalin, Ruth Simmons, and Amy Tsui, as well as Stan Bernstein, helped to clarify the overall focus of the report and provided many specific points and suggestions about additional reference material. Useful comments on the draft were also given by David Adamson, Sono Aibe, Barbara Crane, Julie DaVanzo, Elizabeth Frankenberg, Thomas Merrick, Elaine Murphy, Karen Newman, Sally Patterson, Steven Sinding, J. Joseph Speidel, Ellen Starbird, and Susan Watkins.

Many others kindly provided references and/or copies of materials including Susan Adamchak, Vicky Berry, Jane Bertrand, Joseph Chamie, Harry Cross on India, Leslie Curtin on Indonesia, James Foreit, Karen Hardee and Baochang Gu on China, Judith Helzner, Jeff Jordan, Miriam Labbok, Zuali Malsawma, Penelope Mastt, Susan Palmore, Luis Rosero-Bixby, John Ross, Myriam Sarco on Peru, Sidney Shuler, Martin Vaessen, Ann Way, Neil Zimmerman, and Anatoly Zoubanov.

Special appreciation is given to Julie DaVanzo for her insightful direction and patience. Finally, thanks are also given to Robert Tucker for his support and understanding.

The summary was drafted by David Adamson, RAND communications analyst. The manuscript was copyedited and prepared for publication by Steve Baeck.

AIDS	Acquired immune deficiency syndrome
APROFAM	Asociación Pro-Bienestar de la Familia (Guatemala)
CBD	Community-based distribution
CDC	Centers for Disease Control and Prevention
CDP	Contraceptive Distribution Project
CHFP	Community Health and Family Planning
COC	Combined oral contraceptive
CPS	Contraceptive Prevalence Studies
CSM	Contraceptive social marketing
DHS	Demographic and Health Surveys
EC	Emergency contraception
FDA	U.S. Food and Drug Administration
FY	Fiscal year
GNP	Gross National Product
HIV	Human immunodeficiency virus
ICPD	International Conference on Population and Development

IEC	Information, education, and communication
IMSS	Instituto Mexicano de Seguro Social (Mexican Social Security Institute)
IPPF	International Planned Parenthood Federation
IUD	Intrauterine device
KAP	Knowledge, attitudes, and practices
LAM	Lactational amenorrhea method
MAQ	Maximizing Access and Quality
MCH-FP	Maternal Child Health and Family Planning
MOH	Ministry of Health
NAS	National Academy of Sciences
NFP	Natural family planning
NGO	Nongovernmental organization
ODA	Official Development Assistance
STD	Sexually transmitted disease
TFR	Total fertility rate
UNFPA	United Nations Population Fund (formerly United Nations Fund for Population Activities)
UNICEF	United Nations Children's Fund
USAID	U.S. Agency for International Development
WFS	World Fertility Surveys
WHO	World Health Organization

Chapter One

INTRODUCTION

Family planning programs—organized efforts to provide contraception to women and men—were one of the major social and health interventions in the second half of the 20th century. These programs exist in most countries and in all world regions. As of 1998, 179 governments, representing 92 percent of governments where over 99 percent of the world's population lived, supported access to contraception.[1] Governments provide substantial support for family planning, and most users of contraception in developing countries rely on their governments for contraceptive supplies and services, although the private sector, including pharmacies and private organizations, is also an important source of such services. Many of the family planning programs in developing countries have been carried out with considerable support from international donors.

Over the years, proponents of family planning programs have seen the benefits of these programs as similar to those of other development efforts—e.g., in education, or disease prevention through immunizations—in helping to bring about improvements in the well-being of individuals and societies. However, the international movement to promote and support family planning in developing countries as a way to meet the demand for fertility regulation and as a way to lower fertility and population growth has also generated

---

[1]Contraception is the deliberate prevention of conception by any of various methods. The terms *contraception* and *birth control* both mean pregnancy prevention. Family planning programs provide contraception, or birth control. Health service providers often use terms for methods interchangeably (i.e., contraceptive methods, birth control methods, and/or family planning methods).

criticism and controversy. The critics have included, at varying times, representatives of developing countries, social scientists, interest groups such as feminists and women's rights and health advocates, the Catholic Church and other religious organizations, political conservatives, and representatives of the right-to-life movement. Critics of family planning programs have raised a range of political, ideological, ethical, cultural, and scientific issues.

WHY HAVE FAMILY PLANNING PROGRAMS BEEN SO CONTROVERSIAL?

There are two main reasons why family planning programs have been controversial. The first is because they deal with a subject—birth control (and implicitly sexual activity)—that was a sensitive topic for public consideration for most of the last century.[2] The second is because a political movement to promote particular public policies was spawned out of a growing concern about the negative effects of rapid population growth on the economic development prospects of many Third World countries. While this movement had strong support from a number of quarters, it also generated opposition among a number of groups and for different reasons.

Birth control was for many years a taboo topic for public discourse, and it still is a sensitive issue for some. Anything closely related to sex has been considered by many to be a private issue. This was especially true in the United States prior to the 1960s but also has been and is true in many other countries. Support for birth control became a social movement that aroused opposition from the Catholic Church and other religious groups (e.g., some fundamentalist evangelical groups, some Islamic religious leaders) because of their positions regarding some or all artificial means of contraception.

---

[2] "The term 'birth control' was originated prior to World War I by Margaret Sanger in an effort to help legitimize the efforts of women to prevent pregnancy. In the mid-1930s, Sanger and others advanced the term 'family planning' in an attempt to have reproductive health and pregnancy prevention included as part of the public health movement. The term 'birth control' took on a new meaning with the introduction of modern contraceptives in the 1960s (Chesler, 1997)." (Footnote from Adamson et al., 2000, p. 42).

Advocates of the birth control movement included early feminists, who saw birth control as a way to free women from unwanted and excessive childbearing and as a way to give women control over their bodies.[3]

Subsequent controversies over contraception have included concerns about contraceptive safety on the part of women's health advocates and concerns that women, as opposed to service providers, control or determine for themselves its use.

Finally, the debate over abortion has spilled over onto the field of contraception, with some abortion foes extending their opposition to include organized efforts to promote and provide contraception, especially in developing countries.

The international movement to address rapid population growth stirred controversy for several reasons that have both scientific and political dimensions. First, interest in world population growth on the part of some conservationists, demographers, public health officials, and others was originally focused on the study and understanding of contemporary demographic trends but eventually triggered a call for ameliorative action to address the growing geopolitical problem of rapid population growth (Hodgson, 1983; Harkavy, 1995). The advocates of public action believed that population growth would outstrip the ability of Third World countries to feed their populations, have deleterious effects on natural resources and the environment, and impede economic development. Some of these advocates were political analysts motivated by Cold War considerations. Not all analysts of the potential consequences of rapid population growth agreed with this assessment, and those who did not were at odds with the more action-oriented analysts who saw a need for "population control"[4] in rapidly growing countries such as India and China. Some current policy analysts, who are concerned about low

---

[3]Some early proponents of birth control were motivated by eugenics. In the United States, for example, fertility differences by social class showed that the upper classes were having fewer children than the lower classes, suggesting to some a need to encourage or facilitate lower fertility among the poor. The eugenics movement had largely disappeared by the mid-20th century.

[4]There is an aversion to the term *population control*, once used to characterize policies and programs designed to reduce fertility and population growth, because, for some, the term infers coercion.

fertility, a world population implosion, and population aging in some nations, have questioned whether future population growth and high fertility should remain key public policy issues.

Another reason for controversy was the importance accorded to organized family planning programs as the main public policy for reducing fertility. Early on in the international population movement, proponents decided that organized family planning programs would be an acceptable, feasible, and potentially effective strategy for lowering fertility in a reasonable period of time. Skeptics, including many economists and social scientists, doubted that family planning programs would be so effective; they questioned whether there would be enough *demand* for smaller families and for fertility regulation (the demand-side of programs). Feminists were concerned that the solution to the population problem was being put on the backs of women in developing countries. They thought that investments in other areas, such as education, would create alternatives to prolonged childbearing and rearing for women, and that fertility would decline as the situation of women improved.

Part of the controversy over the role of family planning was the considerable emphasis given to what is called the supply-side of family planning programs. The supply-side refers to organized efforts by governments and private agencies to provide contraceptive services and information to help couples achieve their fertility goals. Those having a supply-side view believed that the main obstacle to increased use of contraception was making sure that methods of contraception were available. Proponents of this view believed that if contraceptive methods were available, women and couples would use them because of their assumed desire for fertility control. Criticisms of the supply-side approach were based partly on the overemphasis given to the availability or supply of services and often focused on the lack of attention to the quality of services in the implementation of family planning programs. Additional criticism came from those who felt that supply-siders did not consider the actual demand for fertility regulation.

The population movement also created controversy because of (1) concerns about cultural intrusion and (2) the conflict between individual human rights and national or societal-level demographic goals. These factors are political and ethical in nature because they involved who was defining the problem and determining the nature of the public policy response, and what means would be used for implementing it. Fears of cultural intrusion were held by many developing countries, at least up to the mid-1970s. Since the proponents of action to address rapid population growth were largely from Western, industrialized countries, some developing countries were suspicious about the motives underlying the population movement as well as how much and what manner of external influence was acceptable or appropriate.

Women's rights and health advocates have been very vocal in pointing to potential and actual conflicts between individual human rights and national demographic goals—particularly goals for fertility reduction that have been part of the demographic rationale for family planning in many countries. While critics hold that governments have a responsibility to provide family planning services, at the same time they contend that the government's role should not interfere with women's rights to contraception; i.e., the government should not dictate or strongly advocate when and what contraceptive methods should be used. The conflict has also involved differences of national sovereignty and individual human rights in those instances where family planning programs have been coercive or heavy-handed in their implementation of population policies and goals.

In light of these controversies and criticisms, the history of family planning programs has been anything but static. Programs have proven highly responsive to the controversies and criticisms, adapting their rationale and methodology at various points, and also generating considerable scientific research, which has greatly deepened our understanding of family planning and fertility-related behaviors, the operation of programs, and the means for evaluating programs.

PURPOSE OF THIS REPORT

The purpose of this report is to examine the origins and evolution of family planning programs in developing countries as public policy. The report looks at the perspectives of governments, donors, and interest groups as well as scientists. Family planning programs have a complex history and have generated a sizable research literature in part because of controversies and criticisms surrounding their development. The report looks at the controversies over the reasons that family planning programs were promoted and the criticisms of how programs were implemented.

The report draws on the relevant research literature to present the current understanding of those concerns or issues that have lent themselves to scientific study. Some of the controversies are based on differing ideologies, where there is little or no scientific contribution possible to clarify the current state of understanding. In these cases, simply describing the different ideological perspectives should be useful to readers.

This report addresses five main questions:

1. What were the origins and evolution of family planning programs in developing countries?

2. What have been the main controversies and criticisms of family planning programs, and were they valid?

3. How has research contributed to understanding whether the criticisms were valid?

4. How have programs changed in response to criticisms and concerns?

5. Through our understanding of the controversies and criticisms of, and the research on key issues for, family planning programs, what conclusions can we draw, what lessons have we learned, and what are the policy implications?

Following this introduction, the report has five additional chapters. Chapter Two reviews the origins and evolution of family planning programs, including an overview of the three primary rationales for programs—demographic, health, and human rights. Chapter Three then discusses the demographic rationale for family planning programs, Chapter Four reviews the health rationale for programs, and Chapter Five analyzes the human rights concerns related to family planning programs. Chapter Six draws conclusions, lessons, and policy implications from the criticisms and the responses to them.

While Chapters Three through Five are organized by major rationale for family planning programs, there is not always a clear-cut distinction or neat fit between the rationales and key controversies, criticisms, and research. Some issues pertain to more than one rationale.

For example, human rights concerns related to demographic goals are discussed in Chapter Three, but they are also relevant to the discussion of other human rights concerns in Chapter Five. Similarly, the broader context of reproductive health for family planning programs in recent years is based on both health and human rights considerations, but the discussion of reproductive health presented in Chapter Four is based primarily on the health rationale.

The purpose of this report is not to review the *value* of family planning programs; that is done elsewhere (e.g., Bulatao, 1998), although this report does review some of the literature on the *effectiveness* of programs as part of the discussion of the demographic rationale for family planning. Nor is its purpose to review what has been learned from the wealth of research that has been conducted on how family planning programs work and what makes for more effective programs, although discussions of cultural sensitivity and quality of care do address some aspects of effectiveness. These topics are presented in other useful reviews (e.g., Lapham and Simmons, 1987; Samara, Buckner, and Tsui, 1996).

Chapter Two

ORIGINS AND EVOLUTION OF
FAMILY PLANNING PROGRAMS

This chapter presents the reasons that family planning programs received growing support internationally beginning in the 1960s; how interest on the part of developing countries governments grew; some of the key characteristics of family planning programs and how these evolved over time; and finally, how family planning programs have been funded—including the level of support from international donors and funding organizations. It provides an historical overview of family planning programs so that the controversies, criticisms, and research related to the rationale for programs, which follow in Chapters Three through Five, can be better understood.

Three U.S. organizations, the Ford and Rockefeller Foundations and the Population Council, served as catalysts in bringing together experts and government leaders from around the world at various international meetings in the 1950s and 1960s to discuss the implications of rapid population growth and high fertility, exchange experiences with family planning program practitioners, and develop a consensus about what was needed for the future (Harkavy, 1995).[1]

---

[1]Two international conferences are examples of these early consensus-building efforts. The International Conference on Family Planning Programs, held in Geneva, Switzerland, in 1965, included participants from 36 countries with representatives from government health ministries and representatives from private family planning organizations, bilateral assistance agencies, international organizations, and private foundations. The First Pan-American Assembly on Population, held in Cali, Colombia, also in 1965, had 80 participants from many countries and called for responsible parenthood by "encouraging couples to have the number of children consistent with

The development of two new methods of contraception—the oral contraceptive pill ("the pill") and the intrauterine device (IUD)—in the early 1960s spurred enthusiasm for making modern contraceptive technology available to countries around the world. Support for family planning was predicated on two assumptions. The first was that women and couples would adopt modern methods of birth control to avoid unwanted pregnancies and to achieve their desired number of children and timing of childbearing. The second assumption was that family planning programs would make contraception widely available and help meet the demand for fertility regulation.

Although there was little experience with family planning programs in the mid-to-late 1960s, there was considerable optimism that they would satisfy several important objectives: to reduce population growth and high fertility and thus improve living standards; to improve the health and welfare of women by helping them to avoid unintended pregnancies and prevent abortion; and to ensure the rights of couples and individuals to plan their families. It is with this backdrop that family planning emerged as an important public health intervention in developing countries and a component of development assistance programs among international donors.

RATIONALES FOR FAMILY PLANNING PROGRAMS

Family planning programs have been a key public health intervention in developing countries and a component of international development assistance programs for three reasons: demographic, health, and human rights. Each of these rationales can also be viewed as goals for family planning programs because each implied achieving certain changes or improvements. The three rationales for family planning have not been equally salient over the entire period from the late 1960s to the present. Concern with the macro-level, or national-level, consequences of rapid population growth on economic productivity, savings and investment, natural resources, and the environment—the "demographic" rationale—was the predominant rationale for much of the late 1960s and 1970s. During the 1980s, a shift toward the health rationale occurred (driven by the

---

their own ideals and compatible with the possibilities available to them for the education and care to which they are entitled" (Berelson et al., 1966, pp. 255–256).

consequences of high fertility for maternal, infant, and child mortality). As will be discussed, this shift occurred in part because of political, ideological, and scientific influences. Among these were that the health rationale was more appealing to policymakers in many countries, including those in sub-Saharan Africa. In the 1990s, the human rights rationale became predominant, with its focus on women's rights, principally reproductive rights,[2] and the reproductive health[3] of women and men. This most recent shift toward reproductive rights as a human right is associated with the United Nations International Conference on Population and Development (ICPD), held in Cairo in 1994.

Demographic Rationale

The history of family planning programs in developing countries partly originates with concern about a "world population problem." In the late 1940s and 1950s, the phenomenon of rapid population growth, resulting from the gap between declining mortality and continuing high fertility, was emerging in some South and East Asian countries. The results from postwar censuses of the early 1950s provided the initial evidence that population growth could be an impending problem. By the mid-1960s, more countries, including a number in Latin America and the Middle East, were experiencing unprecedented rates of population growth of more than 3 percent annually. At such growth rates, the size of a country's population would double in less than 25 years.

---

[2]Reproductive rights include "a) reproductive and sexual health as a component of overall health, throughout the life cycle; b) reproductive decision-making, including voluntary choice in marriage, family formation and determination of the number, timing, and spacing of one's children; and the right to have access to the information and means needed to exercise voluntary choice; c) equality and equity for men and women to enable individuals to make free and informed choices in all spheres of life, free from discrimination based on gender; and d) sexual and reproductive security, including freedom from sexual violence and coercion, and the right to privacy" (UNFPA, 1997, p. 2).

[3]Reproductive health is defined in the UN's Program of Action from ICPD as "a state of complete physical, mental and social well-being and not merely the absence of disease or infirmity, in all matters related to the reproductive system and to its functions and processes" (United Nations, 1995, paragraph 7.2).

Concerns about rapid population growth voiced by demographers, social scientists, and others were based in large part on the assumption that such growth would "serve as a brake" on economic development and on efforts to improve living standards of most of the world's people residing in developing countries.[4] In the late 1940s, conservationists began to write about excessive population growth being a threat to food supplies and natural resources. Some 20 years later, Paul Ehrlich's writings fueled the call to action to deal with overpopulation (Ehrlich, 1968; Harkavy, 1995). Concerns about the impact of rapid population growth and high fertility were translated into what has become known as the "demographic rationale"[5] for family planning. By helping to reduce high rates of fertility, family planning programs were intended to contribute to lower rates of population growth, improved living standards and human welfare, and lessened impact on natural resources and the environment. (The demographic rationale is discussed in more detail below under *Policies and Support of Developing Countries* on pp. 14–19 and in Chapter Three.)

Health Rationale

A second rationale for family planning programs is based on concerns about the health consequences of high fertility held by public health officials and social and political actors, including groups advocating women's rights and needs in developing countries. High rates of maternal, infant, and child mortality (and abortion) were important health problems that required attention. High maternal mortality was associated with a high number of pregnancies, births to older and younger women, and abortions. In Chile, for example, preventing abortion due to unwanted pregnancies was an important impetus for establishing birth control clinics (Romero, 1969).

---

[4]An upcoming report in the *Population Matters* series reviews the relationship between population change and economic performance (Bloom, Canning, and Sevilla, forthcoming). For a discussion of trends in global population growth since the 1950s and the implications of high fertility for economic growth, see Bulatao (1998, pp. 3–20).

[5]The term *demographic rationale* has taken on a pejorative connotation in the past decade, especially as women's groups have criticized national policies aimed at reducing fertility and population growth. These groups assert that such policies place too little emphasis on ensuring women's rights and meeting their health and other needs.

The health rationale for family planning extended to considerations of equity in the access to family planning services. For example, in Colombia, the 1965 founding of the private family planning association, Profamilia, was motivated not only by wanting to help women and families meet their health needs but also by a desire for equity: to give the same access and quality of services to poorer women that wealthier women already had through their private physicians (Seltzer and Gomez, 1998). Class differences in access resonated with the ideological issues of the period such as concern over human rights, which led to the development of major human rights conventions by the United Nations in the mid-1960s. (The health rationale and related research are discussed further in Chapter Four.)

Human Rights Rationale

Family planning became the subject of international human rights when the United Nations issued a statement on population on Human Rights Day in December 1967. The World Leaders' Declaration, signed by 30 heads of government from five continents, stated

> "That the population problem must be recognized as a principal element in long-range national planning if national governments are to achieve their economic goals and fulfill the aspirations of their people.

> "That the great majority of parents desire to have the knowledge and the means to plan their families; that the opportunity to decide the number and spacing of their children is a *basic human right* (italics added).

> "That lasting and meaningful peace will depend to a considerable measure upon how the challenge of population growth is met.

> "That the objective of family planning is the enrichment of human life, not its restriction; that family planning, by assuring greater opportunity to each person, frees man to attain his individual dignity and reach his full potential" (Berelson, 1969b, pp. 7–8).

With this statement, human rights became the third rationale for family planning programs. The following year, the Teheran

Conference on Human Rights, sponsored by the United Nations, affirmed the basic right of couples to decide on the number and spacing of their children. A 1969 General Assembly resolution on social progress and development, called on governments to provide families with the knowledge and means necessary to control fertility (Finkle and Crane, 1975). The World Leaders' Declaration, the Teheran Conference, and the UN resolution helped to legitimize family planning. The issue of women's right to birth control was certainly present at this time in the United States as an element in the women's liberation movement. However, the beginnings of advocacy for birth control were in the 19th century, and the activist crusade for birth control in the United States was launched by Margaret Sanger in 1914 and then spread to a number of developing countries, including India and Mexico, in the 1920s (Douglas, 1970; Dixon-Mueller, 1993).

POLICIES AND SUPPORT OF DEVELOPING COUNTRIES

Today, the consensus among most governments of developing countries is that rapid population growth and high fertility are detrimental to development, and most have policies that favor lower rates of population growth and lower fertility. This consensus came about gradually during the second half of the 20th century as more governments in developing countries faced the consequences of rapid population growth in terms of increasing demands for health and education services, high rates of unemployment and underemployment, and stress on public infrastructure. In addition, the overwhelming majority of all countries today—both developed and developing—favor access to contraception, many through direct government support to family planning programs.

Many national governments have given priority to national family planning programs, in part because of the expectation that increased use of contraception would reduce fertility and population growth. Hence, a growing number of developing countries adopted official policies that include demographic objectives to reduce population growth and to lower fertility (United Nations, 1998, 2000b). Typical of current policies are those for Mexico and India. For example, the Mexican government established objectives in 1995 for the year 2000 to reduce the annual rate of population growth and the fertility rate and also to increase the national level of contraception (Consejo Nacional de Población, 1996).[6] In India, not only does the national government have demographic goals that include eventual stabilization of the population, but a number of states have also adopted official population policies with goals for reducing population growth and fertility, increasing the couple protection rate (contraceptive prevalence rate), and reducing maternal and infant mortality (Department of Family Welfare, Government of Rajasthan, 1999; Department of Family Welfare, Government of Andhra Pradesh, 1997).[7] In general, the population policies and demographic goals for developing countries are part of overall development programs and include, as in India, additional health goals as well as other sector goals.

India was the first country to establish a family planning program. That was in 1952. During the 1960s, a number of governments in other developing countries took an active approach to promoting fertility decline by adopting policies to reduce fertility and population growth and by supporting the development of national family planning programs. The developing countries that did so included (in Asia) Pakistan, Nepal, Republic of Korea, Singapore, Malaysia, Indonesia, and Taiwan and (in Latin America) Cuba, Chile, and Costa Rica (Donaldson, 1990). The rationale for such efforts was a combination of concern about economic development and human welfare. At the same time that developing countries were initiating family planning programs, they were increasing investments in education and health as part of their overall social and economic development efforts.

Beginning in the mid-1970s, the United Nations began surveying governments to ascertain their policies on various population issues, including population growth, fertility, and family planning. By 1976,

---

[6]The government of Mexico first began setting demographic objectives in the 1970s, and thus those set in 1995 were just the most recent of such efforts.

[7]Population stabilization is defined as reaching replacement-level fertility (an average of 2.1 children per woman) by a given year, 2016 in the case of Rajasthan. Even when replacement-level fertility is reached, a population will continue to grow for many years. This is because of a momentum that has been built up in the age structure, due to past high levels of fertility, that has yielded greater numbers of couples of reproductive age who are having children, albeit at an average of 2.1 children per woman.

Table 2.1

Government Policies on the Rate of Population Growth, 1976, 1986, and 1998 (number of countries)

Policy	1976	1986	1998
Raise	28	26	20
Maintain	0	12	16
Lower	39	53	75
No intervention	82	72	82
Total	149	163	193

SOURCE: United Nations (1998, 2000b).

NOTE: The data for 1976, 1986, and 1998 are not strictly comparable because of the changing composition of countries as new ones gained independence over time and other disappeared (e.g., due to geographic reconfigurations). For example, between 1986 and 1998, 15 new countries were added due to the breakup of the former USSR.

39 of 149 countries surveyed had policies to lower their rates of population growth (Table 2.1), and 40 countries had policies to reduce fertility.[8] In addition, 94 countries provided direct support for contraceptive services and another 17 countries provided indirect support (Table 2.2).

Between 1976 and 1998, the number of countries that had policies to reduce population growth increased to 75. At the same time, the number of countries that had policies to reduce fertility more than doubled, to 85. By 1998, the number of governments that facilitated contraceptive use by directly or indirectly supporting access to services had reached 179 of 193, representing 92 percent of governments (Table 2.2). Over 99 percent of the world's population lives in these 179 countries.[9]

The trends in government policies show the consistent move toward greater concern about population growth and support for family planning programs. However, these global trends belie major differ-

---

[8]The 40 countries included the 39 with policies to lower population growth rates plus one additional country.

[9]The combined populations of the 13 countries and the Holy See that provided no support or that limited access to contraception was 43.6 million of the total world population of 6.1 billion in 2000. In addition to the Holy See, these included the countries of Andorra, Brunei, Bulgaria, Equatorial Guinea, Gabon, Georgia, Laos, Libya, Luxembourg, Oman, Switzerland, Turkmenistan, and United Arab Emirates.

Table 2.2

Government Policies on Providing Access to Contraceptive Methods, 1976, 1986, and 1998 (number of countries)[a]

Policy	1976	1986	1998
Direct support	94	116	145
Indirect support	17	23	34
No support	23	18	13
Limits	15	6	1[b]
Total	149	163	193

SOURCE: United Nations (1998, 2000b).

NOTE: See note for Table 2.1.

[a]Government policies on providing access to contraceptive methods "reflect the level of government support for modern methods of contraception (the pill, IUD, injectables, hormonal implants, condoms, and female barrier methods); they are divided into four categories:

a) The Government directly supports the dissemination of information, guidance and materials through government services;

b) The Government indirectly supports provision of information, guidance and materials by non-governmental sources;

c) The Government permits the provision of information, guidance and materials by non-governmental sources but provides no support to such agencies;

d) The Government restricts access to information, guidance and materials in respect of modern method of contraception" (United Nations, 2000b, p. 207).

[b]In 1998, only the Holy See reported that it limited access to contraceptive information and services.

ences among the regions during the 1970s and 1980s. In Table 2.3, we consider whether countries had both an official policy to reduce population growth *and* a family planning program and also whether countries supported family planning for non-demographic reasons, i.e., for health and as a human right.

In 1970 and 1984, the Asian region had the greatest number of countries with both an official policy to reduce population growth and a family planning program. In 1970, the number of countries in both Africa and Latin America with such a policy and support of family planning was relatively small. By 1984, the number of such countries in Latin America had doubled and represented about one-third of the countries in the region. In Africa, the number of countries in this grouping had only increased by two and represented only a small fraction of all countries in the region.

Table 2.3

Developing Country Government Population Policies and Family Planning Programs, 1970 and 1984

Region	1970	1984
Africa		
Policy to reduce population growth rate and support for family planning[a]	6	8
Support for family planning for non-demographic reasons[b]	5	19
Little or no support of family planning and no demographic policy[c]	31	25
All positions	42	52
Asia		
Policy to reduce population growth rate and support for family planning	14	19
Support for family planning for non-demographic reasons	1	3
Little or no support of family planning and no demographic policy	22	28
All positions	37	50
Latin America		
Policy to reduce population growth rate and support for family planning	5	10
Support for family planning for non-demographic reasons	11	11
Little or no support of family planning and no demographic policy	7	11
All positions	23	32

SOURCES: Hermalin (1997) and Nortman and Hofstatter (1980). (The latter is one of a series of publications that ended in 1984.)

[a]Support for family planning means either that the government had established a national program to provide services or gave support to private agencies involved in family planning.

[b]This category includes countries that supported family planning for reasons of health and as a human right, but not for demographic reasons, i.e., to reduce the rate of population growth.

[c]This is a residual category that includes countries that were neutral about their population growth or were pro-natalist.

Through the 1970s, African countries had not viewed population growth as a major factor in their development strategies given the small size of most of the populations (34 of 48 African countries had populations under 5 million in 1978). Not until the 1980s did concern about rapid population growth in the region begin to find public expression (Chamie, 1994). But even then, African governments and international donors found the health rationale a compelling reason to promote family planning. Between 1970 and 1984, the number of African countries that supported family planning for non-demographic reasons nearly quadrupled. By 1998, 38 of 53 African countries had adopted policies to lower the rate of population growth and 50 African countries supported family planning (United Nations, 2000b). Thus, not until after the mid-1980s was there a substantial change in the positions of African governments on population growth. The policy change in Africa reflected the difficulties that many African governments were facing in dealing with high rates of population growth (in excess of 2.5 percent per year for many countries) that were outstripping economic growth and placing heavy demands on governments for health and education services, jobs, and, more generally, on public infrastructure.

The acquired immune deficiency syndrome (AIDS) epidemic has had serious consequences for the health and life expectancy of populations in sub-Saharan Africa. Not only is AIDS the leading cause of death in Africa, but it has also eroded decades of progress in reducing mortality and increasing life expectancy. Because of the increased mortality from AIDS, the question has been raised of whether rapid population growth will continue to be a problem in those countries with the highest prevalence rates of the human immunodeficiency virus (HIV). Nine African countries have HIV prevalence rates of 10 percent or more, and in these countries average life expectancy has declined from 58 to 48 years. Because of high fertility, most countries in sub-Saharan Africa are still expected to grow, albeit at a slower pace than they would have without the epidemic. For example, in Zimbabwe, which has the second-highest prevalence rate of HIV/AIDS infection (one in five adults is infected), the population growth rate is 1.4 percent per year whereas it is estimated that it would be 2.4 percent without AIDS (UNFPA, 1999a).[10] Countries in sub-Saharan Africa are faced with complex policy challenges. They must deal with a devastating epidemic that overtaxes weak public health systems and has very destabilizing social and economic effects, and they must simultaneously meet the demands of still-growing populations.

FAMILY PLANNING PROGRAMS IN DEVELOPING COUNTRIES

Family planned programs exist in most developing countries in Asia, the Middle East/North Africa, Latin America, and sub-Saharan Africa. Over the course of 35–40 years, the number of governments providing direct support to family planning programs has increased from nearly a dozen to 145. Many national government programs are implemented by ministries of health and some by other government institutions such as national social security programs (as in Mexico and Peru). In some countries such as Indonesia, dedicated national family planning organizations have provided services separate from the Ministry of Health. In other places, particularly sub-Saharan Africa, services are integrated with maternal and child health programs. There are also many private family planning programs, the most common being the family planning associations that are members of International Planned Parenthood Federation (IPPF). Private physicians and pharmacies are additional sources of contraception in most countries.

The promise of family planning programs rested on assumptions about couples' desires for children (desire or demand for children) and their desires to control their fertility through the use of contraception (need or demand for contraception). Family planning programs are the organized efforts of government and private agencies to supply contraceptive information and services and thereby assist couples in achieving their desired fertility goals (i.e., both the number of children and the timing of births). It is the combined interplay

---

[10]See Goliber (1997, pp. 28–33) for a discussion of the HIV/AIDS epidemic and its effects on mortality and related socioeconomic and political effects; United Nations (2000a) on the demographic impact of AIDS.

of these demand-and-supply factors that affects the use of contraception and, through it, fertility (Simmons, 1992).

Understanding how family planning programs affect fertility has been the subject of years of study by demographers and other social scientists. A framework for the analysis of family planning effectiveness maps out the social, cultural, economic, organizational, and political influences on the demand for children and for fertility regulation and on related population policies and family planning programs. These influences, in turn, affect other factors, referred to as the proximate determinants of fertility (age at marriage, use of contraception, use of abortion, and breast-feeding) that directly affect pregnancy and childbirth (Lapham and Simmons, 1987). Some of the literature on the impact of family planning programs on fertility is reviewed in Chapter Three.

The following two sections discuss key aspects of the demand for contraception and the supply of family planning services.

Demand for Contraception

This section presents some of the key concepts and measures of the demand for contraception, the sources of information for the measures, and how such information has been used. It also presents trends in the use of contraception in developing countries and reviews the current interest in a measure of outstanding or unmet demand for family planning.

Surveys on the knowledge, attitudes, and practices (KAP surveys) about fertility and family planning were carried out beginning in the 1960s and were important for the development of family planning programs. They collected information on fertility levels and fertility preferences. The preferences of couples, such as ideal or desired family size and whether they wanted more children, were considered a factor in reproductive behavior and perhaps a predictor of fertility and of contraceptive use.[11] The surveys also collected information on knowledge and attitudes about contraception and actual use or interest in using contraception.

The survey results, in general, showed that

- married couples in developing countries wanted fewer children than they were having,

- substantial proportions of couples wanted no more children, and

- substantial proportions of couples approved of family planning in principle and were interested in "learning how to control their own fertility, and would do something if they had appropriate means . . ." (Berelson, 1966, pp. 658–660).

These surveys also showed that a substantial proportion of women did not want to have more children, yet they were not practicing contraception. The discrepancy between women's stated preferences for children and their contraceptive use is referred to as the "KAP-gap" or the "unmet need" for family planning (Westoff, 1978; Bongaarts, 1991). The extent of this unmet need among women of reproductive age provided a basic justification for the development of both public and private family planning programs in developing countries, whose purpose was to provide modern contraception conveniently and inexpensively (United Nations, 1999a). A recent study concluded that "the documented existence of a significant group of women who expressed a desire to limit their fertility and who ostensibly would use family planning services if they were available inspired many governments to initiate ambitious family planning programs" (Casterline and Sinding, 2000, p. 4).

Subsequent to the early KAP surveys, several international survey programs have conducted large-scale national surveys in many countries around the world. These have included the World Fertility

---

[11]In a cross-country analysis of 134 surveys in 84 countries, fertility preferences (the percentage of women wanting no more births) were found to be a valid predictor of fertility and contraceptive use (Westoff, 1990). A recent study in Bangladesh found them to predict abortion as well (Rahman, DaVanzo, and Razzaque, 2001). These findings rebut critics of the surveys who had contended that women did not really understand the survey questions and/or that they did not tell the truth in their responses (Warwick, 1982; Hartman, 1987).

Surveys (WFS), Contraceptive Prevalence Studies (CPS), and the on-going Demographic and Health Surveys (DHS) and reproductive health surveys[12] (Morris et al., 1981; Hermalin and Entwisle, 1982; Cleland, Scott, and Whitelegge, 1987; Robey, Rutstein, and Morris, 1992; Morris, 2000). From 1972 to the present, over 250 surveys have been conducted under these programs (Vaessen, 2000). Over the past 15 years, the national surveys have collected more and more information on existing services and needs for health and nutrition programs in addition to fertility and contraception (see the list on p. 24 of comparative studies that reflects the breadth of information that is contained in the DHS surveys).

These surveys have been used to monitor trends in fertility, contraception, and maternal and child health. For example, governments in developing countries have used information from surveys and censuses to establish goals for reducing population growth, fertility, and mortality and to monitor progress in achieving these goals. The information on demographic and health trends derived from the surveys has provided policymakers and program managers in developing countries—as well as the donor and research communities—with basic building blocks required to assess how well programs are meeting the needs of women, couples, and children on a range of health issues. The information also shows which segments of the population are not utilizing services and can help guide programmatic decisions. Similarly, family planning programs have used measures, such as the prevalence of contraceptive use,[13] to assess how well they are doing. In addition, donors have used data on fertility changes, contraceptive prevalence, and unmet needs for family planning to show whether programs are working and to make the case for continued funding of international population assistance and in policy discussions with leaders of developing countries.

---

[12]The Division of Reproductive Health of the Centers for Disease Control and Prevention (CDC) has been providing survey assistance to developing countries since the mid-1970s. These surveys, now referred to as reproductive health surveys, are one part of a program of assistance under an interagency agreement between CDC and USAID.

[13]The prevalence of contraceptive use is typically defined as the percentage of currently married women of reproductive ages (15–49) who were using a method of contraception at the time of the survey.

Topics of Comparative Studies
from the Demographic and Health Surveys[a]

Fertility and Marriage
Fertility Levels, Trends, and Differentials
Women's Reproductive Preferences
Men's Fertility, Contraceptive Use, and Reproductive Preferences
Socioeconomic Differentials in Fertility
Childbearing Attitudes and Intentions
Gender Preferences for Children
Marriage and Entry into Parenthood

Contraception
Contraceptive Knowledge, Use, and Sources
Unmet Need and the Demand for Family Planning

Maternal Health
Maternal Health Care
Maternal Nutritional Status
High-Risk Births and Maternity Care
Postpartum Effectiveness of Breast-feeding

Child Health
Infant and Child Mortality
Childhood Morbidity and Treatment Patterns
Children's Nutritional Status
Childhood Immunization
Breast-feeding and Complementary Infant Feeding

Health Services
Availability of Family Planning, Maternal, and Child Health Services

SOURCE: Macro International Inc. (1999). See the DHS+ Web site for a list of additional reports based on the survey data (www.macroint.com).

[a]Information has been collected on other topics (e.g., STDs and HIV/AIDS, including knowledge of modes of transmission, symptoms, and use of condoms; and female circumcision). No comparative reports have been prepared on these topics to date.

Trends in contraceptive prevalence in developing countries show an increase from an average of about 10 percent of couples in the mid-1960s to well over 50 percent in the late 1990s (Ross, Stover, and Willard, 1999). Trends by country, as shown in Table 2.4, demonstrate substantial increases and a relatively high level of "met" demand for contraception in many countries in all regions except sub-Saharan Africa. A number of countries have achieved levels of contraceptive use of nearly 50 percent or more. Eleven of 19 Asian countries shown in Table 2.4 have levels of prevalence of more than 50 percent (Bangladesh, China, Hong Kong, Indonesia, Republic of Korea, Mongolia, Singapore, Sri Lanka, Taiwan, Thailand, and Vietnam), but use rates remain low in some of the others (e.g., 13 percent in Cambodia and 18 percent in Pakistan). Among Latin American countries, 15 of 18 (all but Bolivia, Guatemala, and Haiti) have achieved contraceptive prevalence of 50 percent or more. In the Middle East/North Africa region, 7 of the 15 countries have a level of contraceptive prevalence of 50 percent or more. These are Algeria, Egypt, Iran, Jordan, Morocco, Tunisia, and Turkey. However, rates were low in Iraq (14 percent in 1989) and the Sudan (10 percent in 1993). In sub-Saharan Africa, however, only Cape Verde, Mauritius, South Africa, and Zimbabwe have contraceptive prevalence over 50 percent. Rates are below 10 percent in 12 of the 36 countries shown in Table 2.4.

Not only are the levels of contraceptive prevalence substantial in many of these countries, but also changes over time show considerable increases in relatively few years. Over the course of 15 years, prevalence more than doubled in Morocco. Over about a 20-year period, it more than tripled in Indonesia and more than doubled in Mexico. Over a 25-year period, contraceptive prevalence increased more than sevenfold in Bangladesh. Even in sub-Saharan Africa, where prevalence is generally much lower, it increased by more than fivefold in Kenya in two decades, by 2.5-fold in Tanzania in seven years, and by more than 40 percent in Zimbabwe in 15 years.

The use of modern methods is typically a measure that programs use to capture how effective programs may be in preventing unintended pregnancies. The higher the proportion of contraceptive use that comes from use of modern methods, the more effective contraception should be in preventing unintended pregnancies and in turn in

Table 2.4

Trends in Contraceptive Prevalence and Modern Method Use in Developing Countries
(shown as percentages of currently married women of reproductive age)

Country (survey years)	Earlier Survey Year[a]	Later Survey Year	Modern Method Use at Later Survey[b]
		Percentage	
Asia			
Bangladesh (1976, 2000)	8	54	43
Cambodia (1995)	–	13	7
China (1982, 1992)	71	83	83
Hong Kong (1972, 1992)	50	86	80
India (1970, 1999)	14	48	43
Indonesia (1976, 1997)	18	57	55
Laos (1993)	–	19	15
Malaysia (1974, 1988)	33	48	31
Mongolia (1994)	–	61	25
Myanmar (1992, 1997)	17	33	28
Nepal (1976, 1996)	3	29	26
Pakistan (1975, 1994)	5	18	13
Philippines (1978, 1998)	36	47	28
Republic of Korea (1974, 1994)	35	77	67
Singapore (1973, 1982)	60	74	73
Sri Lanka (1975, 1993)	43	66	44
Taiwan (1980, 1992)	69	82	74
Thailand (1975, 1996)	33	72	69
Vietnam (1988, 1997)	53	75	56
Latin America			
Bolivia (1983, 1998)	26	48	25
Brazil (1986, 1996)	66	77	70
Colombia (1976, 2000)	43	77	64
Costa Rica (1976, 1999)	64	80	71
Cuba (1987)	–	70	67
Dominican Republic (1975, 1996)	32	64	59
Ecuador (1979, 1999)	34	66	52
El Salvador (1978, 1998)	34	60	54
Guatemala (1978, 1999)	18	38	31
Haiti (1983, 2000)	7	28	22
Honduras (1981, 1996)	27	50	41
Jamaica (1976, 1997)	38	64	61
Mexico (1976, 1995)	30	67	59

Table 2.4—continued

Country (survey years)	Earlier Survey Year[a]	Later Survey Year	Modern Method Use at Later Survey[b]
	Percentage		
Latin America (continued)			
Nicaragua (1981, 1997)	27	60	57
Panama (1976, 1984)	54	58	54
Paraguay (1979, 1998)	36	57	48
Peru (1978, 2000)	31	69	50
Trinidad and Tobago (1977, 1987)	52	53	44
Middle East/North Africa			
Algeria (1987, 1995)	36	52	49
Egypt (1980, 2000)	24	56	54
Iran (1977, 1994)	36	70	51
Iraq (1974, 1989)	15	14	10
Jordan (1976, 1997)	25	53	38
Kuwait (1987)	–	35	32
Libya (1995)	–	40	26
Morocco (1980, 1995)	20	50	42
Oman (1988, 1995)	9	22	19
Sudan (1989, 1993)	9	10	7
Syria (1978,1993)	20	40	28
Tunisia (1978, 1994)	31	60	51
Turkey (1978, 1998)	38	64	38
United Arab Emirates (1995)	–	27	24
Yemen (1979, 1997)	1	21	10
Sub-Saharan Africa			
Benin (1981, 1996)	9	16	3
Botswana (1984, 1988)	28	33	32
Burkina Faso (1993, 1999)	8	12	5
Burundi (1987)	–	9	1
Cameroon (1978, 1998)	2	19	7
Cape Verde (1998)	–	53	46
Central African Republic (1994)	–	15	3
Chad (1997)	–	4	1
Congo (1991)	–	8	2
Cote d'Ivoire (1980, 1998)	3	15	7
Eritrea (1995)	–	20	7
Ethiopia (1990)	–	4	3
Ghana (1980, 1998)	10	22	13
Guinea (1993, 1999)	2	6	4
Kenya (1978, 1998)	7	39	31
Lesotho (1977, 1992)	5	23	19

Table 2.4—continued

Country (survey years)	Earlier Survey Year[a]	Later Survey Year	Modern Method Use at Later Survey[b]
		Percentage	
Sub-Saharan Africa (continued)			
Liberia (1986)	–	6	6
Madagascar (1992, 1997)	17	19	10
Malawi (1984, 1996)	7	22	14
Mali (1987, 1996)	5	7	5
Mauritania (1981, 1990)	1	3	1
Mauritius (1985, 1991)	75	75	49
Mozambique (1997)	–	6	5
Namibia (1992)	–	29	26
Niger (1992, 1998)	4	8	5
Nigeria (1982, 1990)	5	6	4
Rwanda (1983, 1992)	10	21	13
Senegal (1978, 1997)	4	13	8
South Africa (1976, 1998)	37	62	61
Sudan (1979, 1993)	5	8	7
Swaziland (1988)	–	20	17
Tanzania (1992, 1999)	10	25	17
Togo (1988, 1998)	12	24	7
Uganda (1989, 1995)	5	15	8
Zambia (1992, 1996)	15	26	14
Zimbabwe (1984, 1999)	38	54	50

SOURCES: Ross, Stover and Willard (1999, Table A.1); United Nations (1999a); ORC Macro (2001); Population Reference Bureau (2001). Data for Costa Rica from University of Costa Rica (Rosero-Bixby, 2001).

[a]For most countries, the earlier survey was carried out under the World Fertility Survey program. A dash is used to indicate that there was no earlier survey.

[b]Modern methods include female and male voluntary surgical sterilization, oral contraceptive pills, injectable hormones, Norplant implants, IUDs, condoms, and vaginal barrier methods (e.g., diaphragms; cervical caps; and spermicidal foams, jellies, creams, and sponges) (United Nations, 1999a).

lowering fertility and preventing abortion. In China, use of modern methods is the same as overall prevalence (83 percent). This is in contrast to Bolivia, where the majority of contraceptive use is by women using traditional methods of family planning such as withdrawal or folk methods; such traditional methods constitute 25 percentage points of an overall prevalence of 48 percent. The percentage of married women of reproductive age using modern contraceptive methods is under 10 percent in 21 of the 36 countries in sub-Saharan Africa shown in Table 2.4.

While the trends in contraceptive prevalence demonstrate the level of met need, unmet need remains an important challenge in many countries. The concept of unmet need has evolved considerably since the initial measure of the gap between preferences and contraceptive use. A number of refinements have been made in the way it is measured; unmet need now takes into account the desire to postpone the next pregnancy (i.e., the unmet need for birth spacing) as well as the desire to limit births.[14]

Recent estimates of unmet need for family planning that combine the needs for birth spacing and limiting births range from 6.7 percent in Mozambique in 1997 to a high of 47.8 percent in Haiti in 1994–1995 (United Nations, 1999a). It has been estimated that, overall, about 17 percent of women of reproductive age in the developing world have an unmet need for family planning, and that satisfying unmet need would help reduce fertility among developing countries from a current overall level of about 4 children per woman to just above 3 children (Sinding, Ross, and Rosenfield, 1994).[15] Based on this estimate, satisfying unmet need would exceed government targets for contraceptive prevalence in some 13 of 17 developing countries that have such quantitative goals. The challenge of responding to unmet need is substantial given the various constraints on contraceptive use that many women in developing countries continue to face. (Chapter Four discusses quality of care, which is one of the constraints.)

---

[14]See United Nations (1999a, pp. 106–138) for a discussion of the evolution of interest in fertility preferences and contraception and measurement issues on unmet need.

[15]Unmet need in China was excluded from the estimate given the high level of contraceptive use and assuming virtually no unmet need.

While the demand for contraception is increasing across developing countries, there are regional differences (Westoff and Bankole, 2000). In Asia, North Africa, Latin America, and the Caribbean, most women who have a need for contraception are already using a method. The great majority of contraceptive users in these regions are doing so to limit the number of births. The percent of unmet need among women from these regions has thus become relatively low (ranging from about 9 to 30 percent). While the demand for contraception and the demand for limiting future births are also growing in sub-Saharan Africa, the level of unmet need is much higher because the use of contraception (whether for limiting or spacing births), although increasing, is still relatively low.

Projecting future demand for contraception is based not only on filling unmet need and thus increasing contraceptive prevalence rates, but also on the increasing numbers of women of reproductive age due to population growth. One recent estimate, based on 87 countries, projects that there will be 105 million additional users of contraception between 2000 and 2015, or 79 percent more than the current number of users. These projected "additional users far exceed the number of current users in Latin America and the Middle East/North Africa combined" (Ross and Bulatao, 2001, p. 3).[16]

Unmet need has become a useful concept that bridges both national demographic goals for fertility reduction and individuals' rights (Sinding, Ross, and Rosenfield, 1994). The Program of Action of the UN's 1994 ICPD states, "Government goals for family planning should be defined in terms of unmet needs for information and services" (United Nations, 1995, p. 204). Focusing on unmet need and the extent to which individual fertility goals are achieved underscores the increased emphasis given to individual welfare and rights.[17]

---

[16]This estimate is based on 87 countries that are considered "donor-relevant countries" in that they depend on donor contributions, to some extent, for their contraceptive commodity needs. Two large countries, China and India, are excluded from the estimate since they are considered self-sufficient for contraceptive commodity supplies.

[17]Use of the concept of unmet need has nevertheless been the subject of some criticism. One such critique was that "the concept fails to distinguish between women who have little access to contraception and those who fear it, have religious or other moral

Supply of Family Planning Services

In the early days of family planning programs, the supply of contraceptive services was the major concern. Developing country governments, private organizations, and international donors directed considerable effort toward increasing access to services. For years, lack of access to services was seen as the major impediment to widespread use of contraception (Bertrand et al., 1995 [see especially note 1]). Good access was thought to be the key to women and couples' using contraception. Good access implied that contraceptives should be affordable, that services should be within a reasonable traveling distance and time, and that rules and regulations (such as limited clinic hours) shouldn't limit access. Finally, good access presumed that potential users had sufficient knowledge of methods and where to get them. Access continues to be seen as a constraint in many settings, especially in Africa, where the health infrastructure is weak, and among particular population groups such as adolescents. (The discussion of *Quality of Care of Family Planning Programs* on pp. 82–99 also refers to sociocultural barriers to access.)

Family planning programs are complex systems that convert financial resources, political support and related policy goals, program structure, and management and leadership abilities into programs that provide services (Hermalin, 1997). The general environment in which programs are working also influences them, and many factors can serve to constrain the development and functioning of programs (Simmons and Simmons, 1987). The actual delivery of services depends on human resources (numbers and type of staff, as well as levels of expertise), training and supervision of staff, the availability of contraceptive and other supplies, and monitoring systems and evaluation.

---

objections, or have their decisions made for them by husbands or parents-in-law" (Caldwell and Caldwell, 1997, p. 23).

Table 2.5

**Number of Countries by Strength of Family Planning Program,
1972 and 1994[a]**

Date	Strong	Moderate	Weak	Very Weak or None	Total Number of Countries
1972	8	11	9	49	77
1994	14	32	30	1	77

SOURCE: Ross and Mauldin (1996).

[a]The 30 components of family planning programs that were used to derive overall program strength are described in Table 3 of Bulato (1998).

Given the multiplicity of factors that constitute service delivery programs, it is not surprising that there is wide variation in the strength of programs (see Table 2.5). In a comparative analysis of 77 family planning programs in developing countries, 8 were considered strong in 1972 compared with 14 in 1994.[18] The number of programs considered to be moderately strong increased almost threefold from 11 to 32. The number of weak programs increased from 9 to 30. Most of the increase in weak programs came from countries that either had no program or a very weak program in 1972. By contrast, the number of countries with no program or a very weak one fell from 49 to 1 (United Arab Emirates).

There is variation among regions in the strength of programs. By 1994, almost all programs in East Asia were strong or moderate. In South and Southeast Asia, more than half the programs were strong or moderate. In Latin America, two of every five programs were so considered. For countries in North Africa and the Middle East, however, only one in five were considered strong or moderate. For sub-Saharan Africa, none were considered strong, and fewer than one in six were seen as moderately strong.

---

[18]The relative strength of programs or program effort is based on 30 measures representing four categories of program components: policy, service, record keeping, and method availability. A total maximum score on all 30 measures is 120; strong programs have a score of 80 or more; moderate programs have scores of 55–79; weak programs have scores of 25–54; and very weak or nonexistent programs have scores of under 25 (Ross and Mauldin, 1996).

One of the important characteristics of family planning programs that has evolved over the years is the emphasis on different service delivery channels. Through pilot and experimental programs, it gradually became accepted wisdom that stronger programs needed to have multiple service delivery channels as a way to make services more available to a client population. Typically, the earliest programs began as clinic-based services with a relatively small number of contraceptive methods including the pill, IUDs, and female sterilization. Given that many potential clients did not have access to clinic services, community-based distribution or delivery (CBD) of family planning services using trained outreach workers began to develop in the 1960s and early 1970s. The "purposes [of the CBD efforts] were to make services easily available at the village or even household level, to make them more acceptable by reducing the social distance between provider and consumer. . ." (Ross et al., 1987, p. 343). Various CBD approaches have been carried out over the years in Asia, Latin America, and Africa in order to bring services into the communities where people lived and thus to bring the services closer to potential users. The door-to-door approach in Bangladesh is perhaps the best studied of the CBD programs. (See the discussion of this program in Chapter Five.)

Another channel for service delivery that was tested, first in India in the 1960s and then in Colombia and Sri Lanka in 1973 and 1974, was contraceptive social marketing (CSM). CSM programs "distribute contraceptives through existing commercial and retail channels (particularly pharmacies) and, because of subsidies from national governments or donor agencies, sell them at low prices, with the primary aim of achieving high distribution among low-income groups" (Sheon, Schellstede, and Derr, 1987, p. 367). One assumption underlying CSM programs is that they help to make supplies more widely available than would be possible through only clinic-based services. Further, it is assumed that there is group of potential users who lack access to free or very low priced contraceptives from government outlets, and who are also unable for economic reasons to purchase contraceptives, such as condoms, the pill, and spermicides, at regular retail prices through pharmacies or private doctors. As of 1999, there were social marketing programs in 53 countries in

Africa, Asia, and Latin America.[19] Major contraceptive social marketing programs were operating in 27 developing countries (11 in Asia, 11 in Africa, and 5 in Latin America) (DKT International, 2000).

The range of available contraceptive methods is another facet of the evolution of family planning programs. While early programs in the 1960s relied mostly on IUDs, the pill, and sterilization, advances in contraceptive technology have increased the number, efficacy, and safety of modern methods that are available in many developing countries. Improvements in a number of methods have had positive consequences for contraceptive choice given the differing interests and needs of individuals and couples. There are safer and more effective IUDs. Of hormonal contraceptives, there are safer formulations with fewer side effects, the progestin-only pill that is appropriate for use by breast-feeding women, and different delivery modes (mini-pill, injectables, and most recently, the Norplant implant). There are simplified and safer means of both female and male sterilization, and higher quality and stronger condoms for men as well as the new female condom.[20] There are improved approaches to natural family planning and the lactational amenorrhea method (LAM).[21] The newest method, emergency contraception (EC)—often called the "morning-after pill"—consists of hormonal pills taken after unprotected sex. Its promotion in developing countries began only in 1995.[22] In general, family planning programs have benefited from the availability of this wider range of simpler and safer modern methods. However, as will be discussed (in Chapter Four, under *Quality of Care in Family Planning Programs*, on pp. 88–91), not all programs

---

[19]There were also small programs in Albania, Romania, and Russia that were started in 1995 or later.

[20]The U.S. Food and Drug Administration (FDA) approved the female condom in 1993 (Gardner, Blackburn, and Upadhyay, 1999).

[21]Natural family planning (NFP) refers to methods in which a couple avoids sexual intercourse during the fertile phase of a woman's menstrual cycle (the time in which a woman can get pregnant) to prevent pregnancy or has intercourse during the fertile phase to try to achieve pregnancy. There are a number of NFP methods such as calendar, rhythm, and basal body temperature. LAM refers to the use of breastfeeding as a contraception method and is based on the physiologic effect of infant suckling to suppress ovulation.

[22]This method is not actually new since it depends on use of existing hormonal pills. What is new is information on and promotion of EC as a morning-after pill (Pillsbury, Coeytaux, and Johnston, 1999).

provide and promote a wide range of methods, and clients' needs have not always been of sufficient concern in some programs.

Availability of various modern methods of contraception depends on many aspects of the organization of service delivery, but a reliable and adequate supply of contraceptive commodities such as condoms, pills, injectables, and IUDs is among the most basic factors. Stronger family planning programs have been those with good commodity and logistics systems. Over the years, international donors have played a very important role in supplying contraceptive commodities. Donors and other international organizations continue to assist in the effort to secure contraceptive and reproductive health commodities.[23] While the public sector in a number of countries, such as China and India, funds the supply of contraceptive commodities, most countries remain dependent on donor contributions for their supply needs. Current projections of contraceptive commodity needs for the next 15 years forecast an almost certain shortfall between growing contraceptive needs and the likely response on the part of donors. The growth in the required level of funding to meet projected needs is just over 5 percent per year and represents the combination of increased needs due to growth in the number of women of reproductive age, expected increases in contraceptive prevalence, and the special demands placed on condom supplies in response to the HIV/AIDS epidemic (Ross and Bulatao, 2000).

The historical relationship between the delivery of family planning services and a broader array of services that includes maternal and child health or reproductive health is another aspect of the evolution of programs. Several early government programs, such as those in India, Thailand, and South Korea, placed family planning services within the public health sector, although other government programs in countries such as Indonesia, Pakistan, and the Philippines

---

[23]Under the Global Initiative on Reproductive Health Commodity Management, UNFPA is assisting countries to determine how to meet their contraceptive and reproductive health commodity needs (UNFPA, 1999a, Box 22, p. 52). An Interim Working Group on Reproductive Health Commodity Security, formed in 2000 in response to the UNFPA initiative, is also helping to identify problems with commodity supplies and working with donors, developing country governments, technical agencies, and NGOs to secure essential supplies (Interim Working Group on Reproductive Health Commodity Security, 2001).

created autonomous agencies. By the mid-1980s, the consensus among many nations and international organizations was that specialized population activities (i.e., family planning programs) were legitimate if they were tied to the health and development sectors (Simmons and Phillips, 1987, p. 186). In assessing whether integrated services were more acceptable and led to greater adoption of contraception, the empirical evidence showed that "client populations have responded well to both integrated and vertical services. The lesson appears to be that people desire good services, irrespective of their specific combination" (Simmons and Phillips, 1987, p. 204).

The issue of integrated services was raised again when the "appropriate constellation of services" became an element for improving the quality of care of family planning services (Bruce, 1990).[24] What constitutes an appropriate constellation of services depends on the setting, particularly on clients' needs and what other services are available. In Africa, where health care services are generally minimal, the acceptable context for family planning is generally within maternal and child health programs. Since ICPD, the emphasis on reproductive health as the appropriate constellation of services has given renewed attention to the issue of integration. Empirical studies of the reproductive health approach to the delivery of services will help determine what combination of services is feasible and most effective. (See discussion in Chapter Four on reproductive health.)

FUNDING OF FAMILY PLANNING PROGRAMS

International donors and funding organizations have played very significant roles in promoting interest in population and family planning programs in developing countries. They have also provided substantial support for the implementation and improvement of programs over the years. Developing countries themselves have contributed substantial resources, estimated to be about 75 percent of total funding for population activities in the 1990s. This section highlights trends in development assistance for population programs, discusses the role of developing country governments, and presents brief descriptions of four of the more influential organiza-

---

[24]Concern about the lack of attention to quality of care in family planning programs is discussed in Chapter Four, followed by a review of research on quality of care.

tions: the U.S. Agency for International Development (USAID), the United Nations Population Fund (UNFPA),[25] IPPF, and the World Bank.

Development assistance for population and family planning on the part of donor governments grew from just two countries (the United States and Sweden) before 1968 to 21 by the mid-1990s (Conly and de Silva, 1998). Total funding for population and family planning by donor governments increased from $13.6 million in 1965 (Donaldson, 1990) to $980 million in 1994 (United Nations Population Fund, 1999b). In 1994, four countries provided nearly 75 percent of the international population assistance funds, with the United States heading the list followed by Germany, Japan, and the United Kingdom. Beginning in 1995, the definition of population assistance was broadened to include reproductive health; hence data on funding for population assistance in recent years are not comparable to those for earlier years. Funding in the years following the ICPD increased sharply, reaching nearly $1.4 billion in 1996 and more than $1.5 billion in 1997 and again in 1998 (the most recent year for which data are available). This increase in funding levels after 1994 occurred for nearly all donor governments (see Table 2.6 for trends in donor funding from 1987 to 1998).

Table 2.6 shows that population assistance for these 21 countries and the European Union represented on average nearly 3 percent of Official Development Assistance (ODA), with the United States allocating the largest percentage at 7.1 percent. When population assistance is adjusted based on the donor nations' level of Gross National Product (GNP), the countries that provided the highest relative amounts were Norway ($493 per million U.S. dollars of GNP), Sweden ($356), Denmark ($351), the Netherlands ($313), and Luxembourg ($247). On this basis, the United States ranks ninth in the level of population assistance among donor countries ($73 per million U.S. dollars of GNP).

---

[25]UNFPA was formerly called the United Nations Fund for Population Activities. Although the official name changed to United Nations Population Fund, the acronym of UNFPA remained unchanged.

Table 2.6

International Population Assistance by Donor Countries,[a] 1987, 1994 and 1998 (millions of current $US[b])

Country	1987	1994	1998[c]	% of ODA for Population, 1998	Donor Assistance per million $US of GNP, 1998
Australia	2	18	45	4.6	126
Austria	<1	<1	2	0.4	8
Belgium	1	3	10	1.1	40
Canada	30	23	39	2.3	67
Denmark	16	33	60	3.5	351
European Union	NA	4	79	NA	NA
Finland	9	8	23	5.8	185
France	<1	13[d]	17	0.3	11
Germany	32	115	125	2.2	58
Ireland	0	<1	0	0.0	0
Italy	2	18[d]	6	0.3	5
Japan	54	83	89	0.8	23
Luxembourg	0	<0.1	4	3.8	247
Netherlands	28	44	119	3.9	313
New Zealand	<1	<1	2	1.8	47
Norway	46	41	71	5.4	493
Portugal	0	<1	1	0.5	12
Spain	0	<1[d]	4	0.3	8
Sweden	25	45	78	5.0	356
Switzerland	4	8	18	2.0	64
United Kingdom	26	58	126	3.3	89
United States	267	463	620	7.1	73
Total (in billions)	540	980	1,538	Average country effort = 2.8	67

SOURCES: Conly and de Silva (1998), UNFPA (1999b, 2000b).

[a]Funds were channeled through bilateral programs, spent by multilateral organizations and agencies, and by international NGOs.

[b]Current dollars are the prevailing dollar figures at the time of measurement and were taken as reported by the donor organizations in the UN survey of financial resource flows for population activities (UNFPA, 2000b).

[c]Prior to 1995, UNFPA defined population assistance to include expenditures on family planning services and related public education, population policy development, and demographic data collection. Beginning in 1995, the definition of population assistance was broadened to include prevention of sexually transmitted diseases (STDs),

Private foundations are another important source of funding for population activities, and their support has increased in recent years. In 1998, they provided about $72.5 million or roughly 5 percent of all population assistance. Support from private foundations has increased substantially since the late 1980s when it was under $40 million per year (UNFPA, 1999b, 2000b). Ten foundations provided about 99 percent of the total population assistance from foundations in 1998 (Ford, Gates, Hewlett, MacArthur, Mellon, Packard, Rockefeller, Summit, Wellcome Trust, and World AIDS Foundation). In addition to foundations, a number of nongovernmental organizations (NGOs)—which typically serve as channels of funding from bilateral donors (as in Table 2.6) and foundations to developing countries— have provided funding for population activities, out of their own resources, directly to developing country recipients. In 1998, over $51 million was given by these NGOs. Heading the list were Marie Stopes International and The Population Council. Most of the foundations and key NGOs are based in the United States or Great Britain.[26]

Donor support to international population programs has traditionally been provided through three channels of assistance, with each having about one-third of the funds: (1) direct bilateral assistance from developed country governments to developing country governments; (2) multilateral assistance from UN organizations, primarily UNFPA; and (3) NGOs, including IPPF as well as national and local NGOs in both developing and donor countries.

---

[26]Contributions from foundations have increased since the UNFPA report for 1998, with the involvement of additional organizations (e.g., the United Nations Foundation, funded by CNN founder Ted Turner) and increases on the part of historical donors. Totals may be even higher since not all organizations receive the UNFPA survey on financial resources for population activities, and nonresponse is high from those funding integrated development programs with some population components (Bernstein, 2001).

HIV, and AIDS and also basic reproductive health services such as prenatal, delivery, and postnatal care (UNFPA, 1999b). Hence the trends in population assistance before and after 1995 are not comparable.

[d]In 1994, no figures were reported for population assistance, so this figure is estimated at the 1993 level.

NA = not available and/or applicable.

Reliance on international donor assistance by developing countries was considerable for a number of years, and many countries "came to rely on foreign aid for support of population and family planning projects" (Donaldson, 1990). Gradually, the balance has shifted so that by the early 1990s, it was estimated that three-quarters of all family planning expenditures came from developing country governments (Lande and Geller, 1991). The important funding contribution from developing countries has continued based on a UNFPA survey that estimated governments and national NGOs in these countries spent roughly $7.4 billion on population programs in 1998 (UNFPA, 2000b). This level of funding compares with about $2.2 billion from donors and foundations, and suggests that over 75 percent of funding came from developing countries. The global estimate of domestic resources is impressive, but it belies the fact that the majority of these funds (about 80 percent) came from a few large countries (China, India, Indonesia, Iran, and Mexico). Hence, most countries, especially those in sub-Saharan Africa and the least developed, are still highly dependent on international donor support for their population programs.

The following sections summarize very briefly the involvement of four of the more influential donor and funding organizations.

U.S. Agency for International Development

The largest and most influential of the bilateral population donors has been USAID, part of the U.S. Department of State. The population assistance program of USAID began in 1965 with the announcement that technical assistance in family planning would be available to countries requesting it (Donaldson, 1990). Leona Baumgartner, a high-level USAID official who was also a well-regarded public health physician, spoke near the beginning of the program about international concern with population:

> The goal is increasing movement toward a dynamic balance between the resources, the advancing abilities of people to use resources productively, and the changing number of people who must be sustained by the resources as used. The goal is not reducing, increasing, or stabilizing the numbers of people. It is helping make more possible a richer, fuller life—jobs; homes; resources; freedom from hunger, disease, ignorance; time for development of

innate capacities—in short, enriching the quality of life for an increasing proportion of the world's people (Berelson et al., 1966, p. 278).

The rationale for U.S. government support is reflected in this statement, but was coupled with a strong concern about rapid population growth as a destabilizing factor in international order and a threat to U.S. security in part prompted by the Cold War atmosphere of the period (Donaldson, 1990).[27] U.S. interest in population assistance stemmed from a combination of strategic and humanitarian concerns, including promoting a better life for people in developing countries and enabling couples and individuals to decide freely on the size of their families (USAID, 1982).

By 1968, USAID was the primary source of funding for international population and family planning activities, with a budget of nearly $35 million, representing over 66 percent of the total international population assistance (Donaldson, 1990). By 1994, the USAID budget for population and family planning activities had reached $463 million and was 47 percent of total international population assistance. USAID population assistance is provided to over 80 countries, although roughly half of its funding supports activities in about 20 countries. In fiscal year (FY) 2001, the budget was $425 million.[28]

United Nations Population Fund

Established in 1967, the UNFPA became the dominant multilateral organization and the largest and most influential UN organization in

---

[27]A report in the RAND *Population Matters* series, entitled *The Security Dynamics of Demographic Factors*, reviews the international and U.S. national security implications of demographic factors (Nichiporuk, 2000).

[28]Using the UN's broader funding definition for reproductive health (which encompasses both traditional population support and other elements of reproductive health such as prevention of STDs, HIV, and AIDS), USAID funding for these activities peaked in 1997 at $662 million (UNFPA, 2000b). Using the historic and narrower definition of population assistance, the level of population expenditures reported by USAID after FY1994 declined somewhat, although it was relatively constant, ranging from $426 million in FY1996 to $415 million in FY1999. Only in FY2000 did funding drop considerably, to $373 million (USAID, 2000).

the population field.[29] The United States had been a major proponent of the establishment of such a multilateral fund. Among its purposes, UNFPA was concerned with promoting awareness of national and international population problems and the human rights aspects of family planning. It also provided assistance to developing countries, at their request, for dealing with their needs in the population and family planning fields. In recent years, UNFPA support covers areas such as the integration of population and development strategies, universal access to comprehensive reproductive health services, information and services for young people, and promotion of gender equity and women's empowerment. While most contributions to UNFPA have come from a small number of donor countries, small donations have also been made by many recipient countries, a sign of political support for the organization's work. Some former recipients (e.g., the Republic of Korea) have become contributors. Through 1995, UNFPA provided $3.4 billion in population assistance to 167 countries, and in 1998 it provided support to 155 countries. Annual expenditures for project assistance to developing countries increased steadily over the years, averaging between $100 million and $120 million per year in the 1980s (Conly, 1996) and reaching $328 million in 1996 (United Nations Population Fund, 1999b). In 1998, UNFPA assistance was $284 million. While this sum is higher than the pre-ICPD level of $234 million in 1993, it is 6 percent lower than the peak funding of 1996 (UNFPA, 2000b).

International Planned Parenthood Federation

Among the earliest actors in the international family planning field was the IPPF, which had been established as a private voluntary organization of affiliated national members in 1952 based on the fundamental concern for the rights and needs of the individual and the family. Margaret Sanger, the United States birth control activist who had opened the first American birth control clinic in New York City in 1916, was IPPF's first president (Douglas, 1970). Its membership grew from eight founding members (Germany, Hong Kong, India, the Netherlands, Singapore, Sweden, the United Kingdom, and the

---

[29]Other UN organizations concerned with population and reproductive health include the World Health Organization (WHO), the Joint UN Programme on HIV/AIDS (UNAIDS), and the United Nations Children's Fund (UNICEF).

United States) in 1952 to 137 members in 2000[30] (Berry, 2000). In 1998, IPPF's budget was $90 million, of which about 65 percent was provided as grants to private family planning associations in developing countries around the world (IPPF, 1999). The budget dipped to $83.5 million in 2000 and further to $68.4 million in 2001 because of a combination of factors (Newman, 2000b).[31] The sources of IPPF's funding have included a wide range of governments, international organizations, and foundations.

World Bank

The World Bank became active in the population field in the late 1960s. The Bank has provided funding for population assistance through loans, not grants as with other donors. The least-developed nations have been eligible for very low interest loans with long payback periods, so these funds have functioned more like grants than loans. In the first decades of World Bank assistance in population, the primary concern was reducing high rates of population growth that were seen as detrimental to development. The first Bank loan in population was to Jamaica in 1970 (Harkavy, 1995). In the 1970s, World Bank loans supported the development of facilities and skills to carry out large-scale public-sector family planning programs. During the 1980s, the focus of lending expanded to include primary

---

[30]There are 137 members including the Caribbean Family Association, which itself has 18 affiliates. IPPF thus works with a total of 154 countries. In addition, the organization works with nonmember organizations in about 28 other countries.

[31]These factors, which are instructive for the current fund-raising environment, include a general decline in the official development assistance of IPPF key donor countries, competing priorities for these funds (e.g., Kosovo, a priority for some European donor countries), and population and reproductive health getting a decreasing share of development funds. There were also two IPPF operating factors that contributed: (1) the relative strength of the U.S. dollar (which is IPPF's working currency) meant that most of the other major donations that were provided in other currencies, lost value; and (2) an increase in funding going directly to IPPF member associations in Africa, Asia, and Latin America because of more aggressive fund-raising by those associations and an increasing trend for some donors to fund affiliated associations directly (Newman, 2001).

The restoration of the "Mexico City policy" by the U.S. government in 2001 means that IPPF lost $8 million in FY2001 from USAID, bringing the 2001 IPPF budget down to $60.4 million (unless other donors compensated for the loss). For further discussion of the Mexico City policy, see page 83 of this report.

health care, particularly the health of children and women. In the 1990s, the orientation of bank-funded projects shifted to health sector reform and emerging health problems (e.g., HIV/AIDS). Reproductive health and family planning are generally addressed through broader health programs. The World Bank's funding in population through 1980 totaled $401 million for 22 projects and was $1.1 billion for 66 projects in 1982–1991. For the 1992–1999 period, funding for population and reproductive health was over $3.1 billion for 136 projects in 68 countries (World Bank, 2000).

*****

At the time of ICPD, the estimate of the required level of funding from international assistance for family planning and reproductive health programs in the year 2000 was $5.7 billion (UNFPA, 2000a). Only about $2.2 billion was provided in 1998, and prospects for increased funding, except from private foundations, are not great. These estimates include the cost of the increasing demand for contraceptive commodities and other reproductive health supplies, which are an essential part of meeting the needs of couples in developing countries. Despite the shortfall in financial resources, new partnerships have been formed by developed and developing countries and governments and private organizations that are committed to continuing improvements in reproductive health among developing country populations.

Chapter Three

DEMOGRAPHIC RATIONALE

This chapter deals with three aspects of the demographic rationale for family planning programs. First is the relationship between population growth and economic development. A related issue is the current concern about future population growth and whether declining fertility rates will lead to a birth dearth in more and more nations. Second is the role of family planning programs as a public policy for addressing high fertility and population growth. Third is the critique of the demographic rationale based on concerns over human rights and particularly the conflict between societal and individual goals and rights.

POPULATION GROWTH AND ECONOMIC DEVELOPMENT

The "demographic rationale" for family planning programs was based on concern with the macro-level consequences of rapid population growth. Contemporary scientific interest in the relationship between population growth and economic development began in the late 1940s and 1950s, although theories on the impact of population factors date to the work of Thomas Malthus in the late 1800s. His *principle of population* was that populations grow geometrically, and, if unchecked, would outstrip resources (which were assumed to grow linearly) and lead to declines in the standard of living and to greater misery. The solution to the population dilemma for Malthus was individual responsibility for family size. His work is often contrasted with the views of Marx, who saw the negative consequences of population growth on human welfare as an inherent characteristic of the capitalist system and concluded that the socialist system would resolve the population and welfare dilemma. The modern equivalents of these contrasting views are those who see rapid population growth as a burden for development versus those who see development as the primary means to bring about lower fertility.

The Coale and Hoover (1958) analysis of population growth and economic development in India and Mexico was influential in framing the understanding of the macro-consequences of population growth. Their analysis and subsequent work contributed to the view that rapid population growth would impede development, especially in the world's poor countries. The analytical approach, based on assessing macro-level consequences, provided the scientific foundation for policies and programs of bilateral and international donors, particularly support for family planning programs. The key questions underlying their analysis were whether lower fertility would indeed promote economic development and, if it did, what role family planning programs could play in contributing to increased contraceptive use and lower fertility.

The controversies over differing views of the link between population growth and economic development were aired publicly at several international conferences sponsored by the United Nations. The 1974 World Population Conference, held in Bucharest, Romania, was the first international meeting of governments to address what some called the world population problem. Those who had inspired the conference (the U.S. government and key U.S. foundations and organizations, and a small number of Western European and Asian countries) had hoped to build consensus on the need for world action to tackle the population problem and to promote efforts to limit fertility through family planning programs (Finkle and Crane, 1975).

While attended by 137 countries, both developed and developing, the conference became the venue for a reaction from the majority of developing countries, including Socialist countries, which held views on the population problem that differed from those of the conference's organizers. The developing countries, by and large, saw population problems not as the cause of underdevelopment but rather as a consequence, and thus what was needed was a redistribution of economic resources between rich and poor countries, or a "New International Economic Order." The position of developing countries was also a response to the Cold War political context. The

Western influences that had inspired the conference and promoted family planning were, in essence, rejected. Instead, most conferees favored the view that "development is the best contraceptive."

Despite the polarization in the debates at the 1974 UN conference, a World Population Plan of Action was adopted by consensus at the conference. The primary aim of the plan was "to expand and deepen the capacities of countries to deal effectively with their national and sub-national population problems and to promote an appropriate international response to their needs by increasing international activity in research, the exchange of information, and the provision of assistance on request" (United Nations, 1975, p. 168). The plan stated that population trends were an integral part of economic and social development. Although family planning was de-emphasized as a strategy for demographic change, it was justified for reasons of health and human rights (Berelson, 1975).

A second UN conference served as another occasion for controversy over the link between population growth and economic development, although the sources of dissension were altogether different from the 1974 conference. At the 1984 International Conference on Population in Mexico City, most developing countries had come to recognize the adverse consequences of rapid population growth (see Table 2.1 for government policies in 1986). They also endorsed the principle that governments should help to make family planning services universally available (Finkle and Crane, 1985) (see Table 2.2).

The controversy aired at this conference centered on the official position of the United States. The U.S. position at the Mexico City Conference placed more emphasis on free markets to promote economic growth and reduce fertility than on government family planning programs. Thus, it called into question one of the key rationales for U.S. population assistance—namely, that reduced fertility and slower population growth would facilitate economic development.

The U.S. position was largely a response to domestic political interests on the part of political conservatives, the right-to-life movement, Protestant fundamentalists, some Catholics, and others (Donaldson,

1990).[1] The academic underpinning for the U.S. position was the writing of a "pro-natalist" U.S. economist, Julian Simon. Simon's message was based on an optimistic belief in the creativity and resourcefulness of man—a belief derived from viewing the history of humankind across the centuries. The central thesis of Simon's *The Ultimate Resource* (1981) is that while population growth may be detrimental in the short run, in the long run (beyond a period of 60 years), population growth, at least moderate growth, would be largely positive and beneficial both for developed and for less-developed countries because it would lead to technological innovations. Although other academics considered Simon's demographic-economic analysis simplistic and his reading of history selective and biased, the book nevertheless influenced U.S. policymakers in the early 1980s (Timmer et al., 1982).

The link between population growth and development sparked controversy again a few years later with the publication of a scientific report issued by the National Academy of Sciences (NAS) on population growth and economic development (NAS, 1986). The report did not provide a definitive assessment of the relationship; rather it reached "the qualitative conclusion that slower population growth would be beneficial to economic development for most developing countries." The report concluded that there was simply not sufficient research evidence to provide a rigorous quantitative assessment of the benefits of slower population growth.

The controversy over the relationship between population and development continued into the 1990s and encompassed concerns about natural resources and the environment. For example, the June 1992 UN Conference on the Environment and Development held in Rio de Janeiro reflected fundamental differences in the perception about these relationships. The official conference document, referred to as Agenda 21, placed the blame for environmental problems on both the production and "unsustainable" consumption in developed countries as well as on population growth in developing countries.

---

[1] The official position reflected one perspective, that of the individuals at the State Department and White House who were attuned to the conservative political currents of the time, but did not reflect the views of the professional population staff at USAID, which continued to see the adverse consequences of rapid population growth as a rationale for the U.S. population assistance program.

However, exchanges among participants in the NGO forum, held in conjunction with the conference, revealed deep divisions, especially between environmentalists and feminists, over the causes of environmental problems and the role of population growth (Harkavy, 1995).[2]

The consequences of the controversy over the relationship between population growth and development led to two different responses. First, researchers have continued to study the consequences of population growth, and the most recent research, discussed below, provides new evidence that helps to clarify the relationship. Second, research on the health consequences of family planning, published in the 1980s, provided strong evidence of the health benefits of family planning. The evidence was fortuitous for international donors and population organizations, particularly in the United States, which sought to emphasize other reasons for supporting population and family planning assistance given that the conservative political environment had challenged the population growth and development relationship. The research evidence on the health benefits of family planning and the heightened attention given to the health rationale for family planning by the international donor community are discussed in Chapter Four.

Recent Research on the Consequences of Population Growth

Despite past controversies over the relationship between population growth and economic development, recent research serves to reinforce assumptions made more than 40 years ago about the effects of population growth. The research evidence on the consequences of population growth on development comes from two bodies of empirical work: studies of the macroeconomic consequences (at the aggregate or national level) of population growth and research on the microeconomic consequences (at the family level) of the number of children.

---

[2]For a discussion of population and environment relationships, see Hunter (2000).

Recent research has shed new light on the macro-level relationship between population growth and economic development (Birdsall, Kelley, and Sinding, 2001; Bloom, Canning, and Sevilla, forthcoming). The empirical evidence for this research is based on (a) countries in East Asia that experienced substantial economic growth due to the combination of declining fertility and favorable economic policies; (b) countries in Latin America that also underwent a demographic transition to lower fertility, but did not benefit from appropriate policies and thus did not have strong economic growth; and (c) sub-Saharan Africa, where populations in general are still growing very rapidly, and this growth acts as a drag on economic growth and keeps incomes low.[3]

These new studies have disaggregated the age structure of country populations whereas previous research generally looked at the links between aggregate levels of population growth and economic progress. The dependency ratio—the proportion of the dependent segments of a population (under age 15 and age 65 and over) relative to the working-age or "productive" segments—is at the core of this new analysis.[4] This research has found that changes in population age structure can matter a great deal for economic growth in developing countries. Changes in age structure have occurred because of fertility declines in a number of developing countries that previously had high fertility. Past high fertility produced large numbers of

---

[3]The average rate of population growth in sub-Saharan Africa is 2.5 percent per year, which means that the population for the region will double in 27 years. Initial signs of a transition to lower fertility are evident in only three countries. In Ghana, Kenya, and Zimbabwe, fertility has declined between 15 and 22 percent in fewer than seven years (Kirk and Pillet, 1998). The potential for economic growth in sub-Saharan Africa is further complicated by the impact of the AIDS epidemic. Between 1985 and 2000, more than 14 million people died from AIDS, causing life expectancy to drop sharply in a number of countries in the region and also reducing the rates of population growth. Deaths from AIDS are already having very deleterious consequences for a number of African economies, since these deaths are concentrated among the working-age population (Bloom, Canning, and Sevilla, forthcoming).

[4]The dependency ratio is used as an indicator of the economic burden carried by the productive part of a population even though some people defined as "dependent" are working and some included in the "productive" segment are not working. See Bulatao (1998, pp. 9–20) for a discussion of the importance and implications of the dependency ratio.

working-age people, whereas the more recent fertility declines yielded smaller numbers of young dependents. At the same time, there were not large numbers of elderly dependents. This combination produced a window of opportunity in those settings where the working-age population was educated and jobs were available. A changing age structure can create a larger supply of labor or lead to large numbers of elderly who need to be supported. It can change the demand for education and lead people to save more or less. Such changes can make a significant difference to a country's prospects (Bloom, Canning, and Sevilla, forthcoming). Whether the potential for rapid economic growth is realized, however, depends crucially on the conduct of economic policy. These policies must facilitate employment, savings, and investments in human capital.

The second body of empirical research is on the micro-consequences of family size. It is exemplified by a study of children's education in the context of rapid fertility decline in Thailand. The primary responsibility for funding children's education falls directly on parents in Thailand. As a result, other things the same, the fewer children in a family, the greater the resources available per child and thus the more that can be invested in the education of each child. Smaller family size in this setting was associated with a greater likelihood that a child would stay in school beyond the compulsory years of primary school (Knodel, Havanon, and Sittitrai, 1990). The results of this study provided additional evidence, at the family level, of the positive effect of lower fertility on one key aspect of development: children's education.

In summary, the new studies of the macro-consequences have concluded that there was an important "demographic bonus" for a number of countries, particularly Taiwan and others in East Asia, due to the combination of substantial fertility decline and sound macroeconomic policies. The study of the micro-consequences of family size has shown the benefit of lower fertility for children's education. These studies reinforce assumptions made several decades ago about the links between population growth and development.

FUTURE POPULATION GROWTH OR IMPLOSION

The impressive declines in fertility in many nations in the past half century have led some commentators on public policy to sound an alarm about below-replacement fertility[5] and "populations in decline" (Wattenberg, 2001) and population implosion (Eberstadt, 2001). It is true that the world's rate of population growth has declined since its peak level of just over 2 percent per year in the late 1960s to an average of 1.3 percent for 1995–2000. However, a growth rate of 1.3 percent means that about 80 million people are added to the world's population each year. This is equivalent to adding a country roughly the size of the Philippines or Germany. The world population is estimated at over 6.1 billion in 2001. Both the United Nations and the U.S. Bureau of the Census project that the world's population may reach close to 8 billion by 2025 and over 9 billion by 2050 (United Nations, 2001; U.S. Bureau of the Census, 1999).

While global population growth is projected to continue well into the 22nd century, there are great variations among regions and countries in the annual rate of population growth and in levels of fertility. Eastern Europe (which includes Russia, Ukraine, and Poland) is experiencing negative growth of –0.5 percent per year. Both the Northern and Western Europe regions are virtually at zero growth (0.1 percent per year). In contrast, sub-Saharan Africa (including Egypt, Congo, Ethiopia, and Nigeria) is growing at 2.5 percent per year. South Central Asia (which includes Bangladesh, India, Iran, and Pakistan) is growing at 2.1 percent per year. Given the regional and country differences, nearly all of the world's population growth (99 percent) is occurring in developing countries (Population Reference Bureau, 2001).

The decline in global and regional population growth is due to declining fertility in most nations. Just as with population growth rates, there is considerable variation in fertility trends. Levels of fertility, measured by the total fertility rate (TFR), have declined most rapidly

---

[5]Below-replacement level is the level of fertility at which a cohort of women (i.e., a particular group of women who share a common temporal experience, often defined in terms of an age group such as women ages 20–24) on average are not having enough daughters to "replace" themselves in the population. A total fertility rate (TFR) of 2.1 children per woman is considered to be replacement level; thus a TFR below 2.1 is below replacement fertility.

in Latin America and Asia.[6] Fertility fell in Asia over the past 50 years from 5.9 to 2.6 children per woman (largely driven by a sharp decline in China to 1.8) and from 5.9 to 2.7 in Latin America. While there has been some decline in sub-Saharan Africa, it has been much smaller—from 6.5 to 5.5 children per woman—and the decline has occurred more recently. Fertility in Europe fell over the past 50 years from about 2.6 to 1.4 children per woman, a level well below replacement (UNFPA, 1999).

This varied picture of population growth and fertility means that the world as a whole and many nations, especially those in developing countries, will experience continued population increase for many years to come. It also means that a number of countries, especially more developed ones (including Japan and South Korea in East Asia and France, Germany, Italy, the United Kingdom, and Russia in Europe), are slowly diminishing in population size, assuming current rates of fertility remain below replacement. Low fertility, low mortality, and longer life expectancy also mean that these populations are aging, i.e., that the average age of the population is increasing. Adjusting to an aging population is one of the demographic challenges facing a small but growing number of developed countries. For most of the world's countries, the major demographic challenges over the next several decades will continue to involve reducing mortality and fertility through a combination of economic growth and social sector programs, including those in education and health.

ROLE OF FAMILY PLANNING PROGRAMS

The appropriate role of family planning programs, including contraceptive technology, in addressing high fertility and rapid population growth has been a continuing source of debate since the 1960s among public health officials, social scientists, feminists, women's health advocates, and scientists involved in the development and introduction of new contraceptives. With the introduction of two new contraceptives in the early 1960s—the pill and the IUD—there was much enthusiasm about the potential contribution of contraceptive

---

[6]The TFR is the average number of children that would be born alive to a woman (or a group of women) during her lifetime if she were to pass through all her childbearing years experiencing the age-specific fertility rates of that year.

technology. According to one analyst of the early years of family planning programs in developing countries, "Defining the population problem in terms of a lack of contraceptive supplies . . . [enabled international donor agencies] to intervene quickly, cheaply, and without much attention to local circumstances. . . . Moreover, a tech-nological fix to the problem of high fertility and rapid population growth must have been particularly appealing to public health practitioners and policymakers who saw the impact that technology—for example, spraying for mosquitoes—had on mortality rates in developing countries" (Donaldson, 1990, p. 55). Family planning programs were the public policy intervention for delivering contraception, and "public health professionals [who] understood the possibilities of well-planned, carefully targeted intervention" readily supported the development of these programs (Donaldson, 1990, p. 59).

A number of social scientists found family planning much too narrow an approach to address concerns about high rates of population growth and fertility. They were critical of international donors and especially the United States for the strong focus on family planning and contraceptive supplies. The suspicions of some social scientists about a contraceptive-based solution to the population problem were founded on their understanding of the complex cultural and social influences on childbearing in traditional societies. They doubted that there was enough demand among families for fertility control; they thought that family planning programs could not influence fertility preferences and thus bring about changes in high-fertility countries (Davis, 1967). They considered that even if family planning were to enable all couples to have their desired number of children, many couples would continue to want and have many children, and high fertility would continue to fuel a level of population growth that would undercut development efforts. Thus, these scientists believed that family planning would be insufficient to help resolve "conflicts between the fertility goals of individual couples and the demographic goals of the society" (Donaldson, 1990, pp. 57–59).

Such social scientists believed that what was called for were policies, including fertility policies that went "beyond family planning," and economic and social development. Such fertility policies might include anti-natalist incentives such as pensions given to parents who choose to have a small number of children or the withdrawal of maternity benefits after a certain number of children. Other broader development policies might include those aimed at changing social and economic institutions in ways that would lead to lower fertility. These might include, for example, increasing the minimum age of marriage, encouraging women to work in the labor force and outside the home, and supporting improved and universal education. It was believed that such policies would change the motivation or incentives for families to have many children (Berelson, 1969a; Demeny, 1992).

One of the consequences of the skepticism by social scientists about the role of family planning as a public policy for reducing fertility has been the extensive research on the design, management, financing, and evaluation of family planning programs (Lapham and Simmons, 1987; Phillips and Ross, 1992; Buckner et al., 1995). Part of this research has been devoted to developing techniques for evaluating programs. Evaluation methods have evolved as the nature and structure of programs have changed and become more complex (Hermalin, 1997). A summary of some of this research is below, under *Research on the Effectiveness of Family Planning Programs.*

Feminists, too, were critical of the emphasis given to family planning as a key instrument of population policy to lower fertility. They favored broader development approaches to transform the condition of women in developing countries. Social and economic investments directed toward women were seen not only as having the potential to enhance the status of women, but also as a way to lower fertility by giving women alternatives to prolonged childbearing and rearing. Many of these critics saw the narrow focus on family planning and contraception as insufficient to meet women's needs (Hartman, 1987; Germain and Ordway, 1989; Dixon-Mueller, 1993). In general, these critics held that if family planning programs were genuinely concerned about women's needs and welfare, then addressing their needs within the broader context of reproductive rights and health should be a priority. The response to this concern is discussed in Chapter Four.

Research on the Effectiveness of Family Planning Programs

Proponents of family planning programs as the primary public policy assumed that these programs would help to bring out a decline in fertility. The validity of this assumption can be assessed by looking at the research evidence that has accumulated over many years. Programs are thought to affect fertility by offering improved services that lead to reductions in unmet need, which in turn help to decrease the level of unwanted fertility, and ultimately result in lower fertility (Bongaarts, 1995). Programs are thus thought to help reduce the "cost" of achieving desired family size. The large literature evaluating the impact of family planning programs on fertility shows that the task has been quite complex, and that there are no simple answers.

What does the research show? Worldwide, fertility has declined substantially. The average number of children born to a woman has decreased from about six in the mid-1960s to fewer than three today (Robey, Rutstein, and Morris, 1992; Population Reference Bureau, 2001).[7] Contraceptive use has increased from 10 to 60 percent (Population Reference Bureau, 2001). Over this period, there have been improvements in the social and economic conditions in many countries as well as changes in political systems, in cultures, and in the nature of communication; these various changes played a part in fertility decline. What has been the role of family planning programs in the changes in fertility?[8]

There have been different approaches to assessing the impact of family planning programs. One involves a series of studies that compares countries, using aggregate data on fertility levels, the strength of family planning programs (program effort), and the level of social and economic development over time (Lapham and Mauldin, 1972, 1984, 1987; Mauldin and Ross, 1991). In general, these studies have found that there are both joint and independent effects of program efforts and socioeconomic development on fertility. The studies have shown that a country's level of social and economic development affects fertility in two ways: (1) through its direct effect on the people's behavior, specifically their use of contraception and their fertility, and (2) through its indirect effect on the capability of institutions

---

[7]For 2000, the TFR is estimated at 2.9 children per woman (Population Reference Bureau, 2000).

[8]Bulatao (1998) presents a useful summary of the record of family planning programs in developing countries.

to organize family planning programs (Freedman and Berelson, 1976; Simmons and Young, 1996).[9]

Another study, which used the same measure of family planning program effort but a different measure of development, estimated that fertility in developing countries would have been higher (5.4 births instead of the actual 4.2 births) for the 1980–85 period if there had been no family planning programs (Bongaarts, Mauldin, and Phillips, 1990). In a subsequent study, Bongaarts (1994) also found clear evidence of unmet need, and further, that unmet need is related to unwanted fertility. He found that family planning programs contributed to a decline in fertility by reducing unwanted childbearing, and that stronger programs reduced unwanted childbearing more. A subsequent analysis concluded that 43 percent of the fertility decline that occurred in the developing world between the 1960–1965 period and the 1985–1990 period could be attributed to family planning programs (Bongaarts, 1995).

The research cited above has helped to point out the complexities in studying the impact of family planning programs and has improved overall understanding, based on cross-national analysis, of the conditions under which programs affect fertility. There have been criticisms of this research and challenges to the study results (e.g., Demeny, 1979; Hernandez, 1984; Pritchett, 1994), but the general consensus held by demographers and social scientists is that both socioeconomic development and program effort cause fertility to decline. However, the amount of reduction achieved by family

---

[9]In the most recent such study, the association between level of development and program effort has weakened, suggesting that socioeconomic factors are less important as determinants of the level of family planning program effort than they once were (Ross and Mauldin, 1996). Furthermore, overall improvements in family planning programs were quite modest for the most recent period examined (1989–1994), which may reflect the fact that donors and some developing country governments have not maintained their previous levels of support. The authors conclude, "A sense of complacency [among donors and developing country governments] may have resulted from rapid increases in contraceptive prevalence and decline in fertility [that occurred in the past]; but these increases may slow or cease unless significant improvement occurs in background socioeconomic conditions, ideational influences, and program effort" (Ross and Mauldin, 1996, p. 144).

planning programs depends on the level of development in a given setting.

A recent analysis looked at the role of family planning programs in the fertility transition in the Latin American region (Mundigo, 1996). In the early 1960s, epidemiological studies showed a high incidence of induced abortion in several Latin American countries—evidence that women were having "excess fertility" and of an unmet demand for contraception. By the late 1960s, survey data showed that "excess fertility" was the norm (i.e., that women were having more children than they considered ideal) for most countries in the region, and there was a real unmet demand for fertility regulation. Gradually, decreases in desired family size and increases in the demand for contraception moved from the upper and middle socioeconomic groups to the lower socioeconomic groups. The analysis concludes that in the fertility transition in Latin America, family planning programs "played an instrumental role as facilitators of the mass transition [to lower desired family size and lower fertility] rather than as the agents responsible for these changes" (Mundigo, 1996, p. 207).

Evidence of the role of family planning programs is also based on pilot and experimental studies. Two such studies in Matlab, Bangladesh, and Chogoria, Kenya, have shown that intensive high-quality efforts can lead to increased contraceptive use and lower fertility even in settings with low social and economic development (Phillips et al., 1988; Goldberg, McNeil, and Spitz, 1989). The Matlab study is discussed in Chapter Five as an example of a culturally sensitive experimental project.

A recent study of fertility change in Bangladesh supports the important role of the family planning program, particularly in the pace of the fertility decline and perhaps in the timing of its onset (Caldwell et al., 1999). However, it argues that there were also important changes in the socioeconomic conditions (e.g., the percentage of girls with any schooling increased from 43 to 71 percent between 1976 and 1996) that contributed to lower fertility. In interviews with Bangladeshi families living in the rural southeast part of the country, this study reported that the respondents "place the greatest emphasis on the contemporary problems and opportunities that their parents, let alone their grandparents, never faced. But they also argue that they are able to control family size because of access to contraceptive methods that were unknown to their forebears" (Caldwell et al., 1999, p. 81).

As noted in a review by Ronald and Deborah Freedman (1992), several country studies have provided evidence of major fertility declines where conditions were considered unfavorable. In Indonesia, the decline in fertility and the rise in use of contraceptives were attributed to the distinctive and effective program strategy even though the program began under rather unfavorable social and economic conditions (Warwick, 1986). In Thailand, where social and economic conditions were considered moderately favorable, fertility declined rapidly and contraceptive use rose markedly (Knodel, Chamratrithirong, and Debavalya, 1987). (The case of Thailand is also discussed in Chapter Five.) Other evidence, cited by Freedman and Freedman (1992), shows that within a country, high prevalence of contraceptive use and lower fertility are associated with greater or high-quality program effort, as in Taiwan (Hermalin, 1978) and Malaysia (Tan, 1987).

A consequence of the interest in evaluating family planning programs has been the evolution in the approaches used to assess impact. According to Hermalin and Khadr (1996), the methods for evaluation have changed in response to changing program structures, new questions, and deeper scientific knowledge. Methods have evolved from those based on "acceptors" of programs (i.e., those people who used a program's services or were acceptors of contraceptive methods) and that try to trace the impact on fertility of those accepting program methods to "population-based methods that incorporate all program effects on the fertility rates of the population as a whole, which may extend beyond acceptors *per se* to incorporate the legitimizing and motivating effects of the program" (e.g., mass media campaigns that promote the practice of family planning) (Hermalin and Khadr, 1996, p. 6). Further, as programs moved beyond the bounds of the clinic setting to incorporate community-based and social marketing strategies for service delivery, using the increasing number of population-based surveys (through the WFS, CPS, and DHS programs) to assess programs has been important.[10]

---

[10]Other reviews of methods for evaluating the impact of family planning programs are Ross and Lloyd (1992), Buckner et al. (1995), and Hermalin (1997).

In summary, family planning programs have been found to be an effective public policy in many developing countries for increasing contraceptive use and lowering fertility. Evidence from aggregate, cross-national studies showed that family planning programs had an effect independent of social and economic development on fertility. In general, the amount of reduction in fertility depended on the level of development in a given setting. In the Latin American region, research concluded that family planning programs facilitated, but did not cause, the transition to lower desired family size and lower fertility. Evidence from pilot and experimental projects, some of which are discussed in subsequent chapters, has shown that high-quality family planning efforts have led to increased contraceptive use and lower fertility.

HUMAN RIGHTS CHALLENGE OF THE DEMOGRAPHIC RATIONALE

Proponents of the demographic rationale for population policies and programs (i.e., the need to reduce fertility and population growth in order to improve social and economic well-being) have included the main constituencies of the international population movement, namely, donor organizations, foundations and organizations with a special interest in population, and over time an increasing number of developing country governments. Critics of the demographic rationale for family planning programs have included women's rights and health advocates, primarily from developed countries beginning in the 1960s but with much greater representation from developing countries since the mid-1980s.

The feminist critique of the demographic rationale for family planning was that women have a right to make their own decisions and to control their bodies without government intervention (Dixon-Mueller, 1993). According to this critique, programs based on a demographic rationale (population control programs) had specific goals for fertility reduction and contraceptive use; they viewed women as numerical "targets" to be filled (e.g., numbers of acceptors of contraception). Given the attention to goals and targets, these programs were seen as being incompatible with human rights. In addition, critics pointed to a number of abuses—such as coercive aspects of some major family planning programs, and a lack of attention to the quality of services—that were a consequence of an overemphasis on population control and too little emphasis on women's reproductive rights and welfare. For some critics, the use of incentives has been another controversial aspect of programs because they see incentives as influencing contraceptive choice (Hartman, 1987). At the same time, others have recognized that the nature and ethics of incentives vary across different settings and that incentives are an acceptable feature of public policy in many sectors. These researchers have identified many complexities (such as setting ethical standards) for determining an appropriate role for incentives in family planning programs (Cleland and Robinson, 1992; Issacs, 1995).

The human rights basis for reproductive rights is the UN's Universal Declaration of Human Rights of 1948 (Dixon-Mueller, 1993). This declaration defined two concepts of rights: (1) certain individual rights that are inalienable, i.e., civil and political rights or personal freedoms; and (2) social entitlements in the sense that society is responsible for ensuring certain welfare or economic and social rights. Based on these two concepts, the state must guarantee not only the freedom of opportunity to its citizens, but also the achievement of results. Applied to reproductive rights, there are two rights: the right to decide freely and responsibly on the number and spacing of children (a civil right) and the right to information, education, and the means for couples to regulate their fertility (a social entitlement). Drawing on the feminist discourse spanning the 19th and 20th centuries, a third reproductive right is woman's right to "control her own body," which was part of the broader process of social transformation and a fundamental means to free women (Dixon-Mueller, 1993, p. 12). Thus according to feminists, governments have a responsibility to ensure reproductive rights and to provide family planning services.

The critique of the demographic rationale has been justified by a number of country examples (presented below) where individual human rights were sacrificed for, or were secondary to, national-level goals. These examples do not represent an exhaustive review of problems with implementing demographic goals, but they help to explain the increased international concern with human rights and reproductive rights in recent years, especially at the 1994 ICPD. The examples of problems should be viewed within the larger context of the many developing countries that have official population policies to reduce population growth and fertility and that do not violate human rights.

National population policies and health goals are used for setting priorities and for planning and budgeting and thus help to determine the allocation of human and financial resources for carrying out programs. These goals are typically translated into goals for family planning programs in terms of the national and sometimes state levels of contraceptive prevalence. The use of such broad goals for planning and budgeting implies no necessary infringement on the voluntary nature of family planning programs. If these goals are the basis for setting targets and quotas for program staff to fulfill at the lowest administrative or program levels—for example, a given number of IUD users per health district or clinic or a given number of women sterilized—then the rights and welfare of individuals and couples may be compromised.

Examples of Human Rights Problems Where Demographic Goals Were Emphasized

The following country examples illustrate some of the problems that have arisen because of the manner in which demographic goals were implemented. In addition to national demographic goals, the rhetoric of some family planning programs has sometimes been ambiguous: insisting on consumer rights or sovereignty for fertility preferences while issuing strong anti-natalist messages (McNicoll, 1997). Each of the national programs discussed below is undergoing modifications partially in response to the ICPD agenda and the increased attention to individual rights and welfare.

China. China established a one-child policy in 1979 in order to keep the total population at fewer than 1.2 billion by 2000. The Chinese population in mid-2000 is estimated at 1.265 billion (Population Reference Bureau, 2000).[11] Despite an official national policy stating that

---

[11]The 1970 population of China was 970.9 million, and the annual rate of population growth was 1.2 percent in 1980, although it had been 2.0 percent per year or higher for much of the 1950s and until 1974. If growth had continued at the rate of 1.2 percent per year, the population would have been 1.6 billion by 2000 (Arid, 1982), or 335 million more than its actual size in 2000.

the family planning program is voluntary, not compulsory, and that people are persuaded but not forced to practice birth control, a system of mandatory fertility control was instituted. Couples had little choice about whether they practiced birth control, how many children they would have, and the timing of births. Family planning contracts that included a one-child pledge were required of couples. Births were either approved as part of the local government's birth plan or they were forbidden and outside the official birth plan. A practice of requiring use of specific contraceptive methods was also instituted, in which women with one child had to use an IUD, couples with two children had to have one partner sterilized, and those with unauthorized pregnancies had to undergo abortion. Thus the primary methods of fertility regulation used to implement the program were sterilization, IUD, and abortion, and women or couples had little choice of which method to use.

Throughout the 1980s, the Chinese program was characterized by regulations, and guidelines were established at the national level and then "prescribed to provincial and lower levels of government and ultimately to couples of childbearing age" (Hardee-Cleaveland and Banister, 1988, p. 277). Family planning was rarely considered a personal matter. China is the prime example of a program driven to achieve collective welfare by reducing population growth, but which sacrificed individual rights and welfare through an essentially involuntary program. While the one-child policy was not uniformly implemented in all areas of China—particular exceptions pertain to rural areas and ethnic minorities—it was nevertheless the driving force of the family planning program (Hardee-Cleaveland and Banister, 1988).[12]

Despite the coercive character of the Chinese program, Chinese women from two provinces who were interviewed in a 1996–97 study

---

[12]To protest reports of coerced abortion in the implementation of China's one-child policy, the United States reduced its annual contribution to UNFPA in 1985 and ceased funding UNFPA altogether from 1986 through 1992. The U.S. government withdrew support because UNFPA was providing population assistance to China at the time (Conly, 1996). The withdrawal of support occurred even though a USAID review found that no UNFPA funds were supporting abortion or coercive family planning practices (Hardee-Cleaveland and Banister, 1988).

viewed family planning as a fact of life, in spite of initial resistance. "Among younger couples, family planning is seen as a societal norm while older women express regret at not having had access to contraception. Older study participants equated larger family size with economic burden, personal suffering and missed professional opportunities" (Barnett and Stein, 1998, p. 55).

Recent program developments, in part prompted by the ICPD, indicate that the Chinese government is allowing some experimentation to set up different models and to reorient the State Family Planning Program by addressing improved quality of services and choice of methods. For example, the Ford Foundation is supporting a Women's Reproductive Health and Development Program in Yunnan Province. The program works through a community-based approach to planning. Provincial and country-level guidance groups were created involving local government, the Women's Federation, and family planning and health officials (Ford Foundation, no date). The UNFPA has also been supporting efforts by the State Family Planning Program to increase attention to clients' needs and quality of care. By late 1999, there were some 660 rural counties and urban districts under the State Family Planning Program that had started reorientation experiments emphasizing quality of care (Gu, 2000).

India. India is another example of a program that, despite its official name (Family Welfare Program), has been dominated for many years by demographic objectives to the apparent detriment of women's rights and welfare. This was so despite the main appeal in the early years of the national family planning program based on its potential to improve the health, especially of mothers and children, and the welfare of the family (Visaria and Chari, 1998). In the mid-1960s, the central government introduced method-specific targets for each state, and state programs were required to fulfill these targets down to the lowest administrative level. Use of targets was also considered an incentive to encourage family planning workers to do their job. Local health workers were ultimately responsible for achieving targets, including method-specific targets, and failure to do so often led to serious salary or job consequences. Because of the pressure to meet targets, these health workers often overreported levels of use or "coerced couples into accepting sterilization" (Visaria, Jejeebhoy, and Merrick, 1999, p. S44).

The Indian program evolved primarily into a single-method program—sterilization—because it was a long-term effective method,
and hence, client choice of methods was greatly limited. During the
"emergency" period of 1975–1977, the central Indian government increased incentives, in the form of monetary compensation, to individuals undergoing sterilization. Public officials also used "ethically
dubious tactics to promote sterilization" including threats to with-
hold one month's pay of schoolteachers who did not consent to be
sterilized (Warwick, 1982). Even after the emergency period and until
the early 1990s, the government vigorously promoted sterilization.

In 1992, the Indian government acknowledged that the program had
not achieved its overall goals primarily because of its centralized
planning and target setting. Since that time and with the added impetus of ICPD, the Indian Family Welfare Program has been in the
process of a major reform. Targets were officially abandoned in 1996,
and efforts are being supported for a more community-based approach to meeting needs in a number of states with assistance from
USAID (Visaria, Jejeebhoy, and Merrick, 1999; Narayana et al., 1999;
Reddy, Hanumantharayappa, and Sathyanarayana, 2000; Dwivedi
and Mangal, 2000; Narvekar, Pendse, and Sathyanarayana, 2000;
Narayana and Rao, 1999). The process of implementing the target-
free approach has not been easy, despite various pilot efforts to do
so. Part of the challenge is to convey to thousands of health workers
all over India that the program "seeks to meet people's health needs
rather than administratively determined targets." The strategy of
conducting community-based needs assessment in theory has great
potential as both a planning and a performance-monitoring tool in a
"target-free" India, but there is, as yet, little actual experience with
these assessments (Indian Institute of Health Management Research
et al., 1999). An additional response to abandoning demographically
driven goals has been the approval in FY1997 of a new Reproductive
and Child Health Project funded by the World Bank. The project
supports various policy changes in addition to the removal of targets
and includes support for states' gradually removing incentive payments to providers and acceptors of certain family planning methods
(World Bank, 2000). The Indian government recently issued its new
National Population Policy 2000, which includes ambitious goals for
reducing fertility. It hopes to achieve these "through 'promotional
and motivational measures' that emphasize quality of life, rather

than through numerical targets for the use of specific contraceptive methods" (Sharma, 2000, p. 6). Addressing unmet needs for basic reproductive and child health services, keeping girls in school longer, and raising the age at which girls marry from 18 to 20 years are additional policy goals.

Indonesia. Indonesia represents an interesting example of a program that has been both lauded and criticized. As one observer has stated, Indonesia's family planning program is a story of competence and enthusiasm as well as co-optation and pressure (McNicoll, 1997). The praise was based on the fact that the program was effective in using the existing government administrative system to mobilize village leadership and also that local community support of contraception by village leaders, their wives, and others helped to legitimize the use of contraception among potential acceptors (Freedman, 1987a). Program objectives that were defined in the late 1960s included "attaining majority acceptance of the principle of family planning, introducing the concept of a small prosperous family, and ensuring that adequate contraceptive services were provided to married couples who wished to plan their families" (Hoesni, 2000). Also at this time, targets for new family planning acceptors were introduced. Incentives were also provided to family planning field workers (the initial monetary rewards were replaced by certificates of merit by the end of 1974) to encourage them to achieve established targets in their respective geographic areas. There were also incentives for communities—e.g., the provision of public services such as wells—and for individuals in terms of certificates signed by the president for long-term users (Hoesni, 2000). Sterilization was never an official program method, because of the opposition to this method on the part of Muslim religious leaders. Hence, incentives or policies promoting sterilization, seen in some other Asian programs, were not part of the Indonesian program.

By the mid-1980s, the program had achieved considerable success with a contraceptive prevalence rate of more than 60 percent. However, questions were raised about how much free choice existed among clients. The strong role of the central authority and the nature of community decisions by consensus meant that individual choice was acceptable as long as it was in harmony with the national consensus (Warwick, 1986).

Over time the initial goal of the family planning program shifted from maternal health to population control. Family planning became part of the government structure using authoritarian mechanisms of social mobilization (Hull and Iskandar, 2000). In 1992, partly in response to criticism from Indonesian women's groups and NGOs, the goal of the family planning program shifted away from the achievement of targets and toward a commitment to fulfilling clients' unmet needs for contraceptive and broader health needs as well (Hull and Iskandar, 2000; Smyth, 1991). For example, one of the quality-of-care issues that generated considerable criticism (referred to in Chapter Four of this report) was the inadequate counseling of women and inadequate training of providers to ensure that women could have the Norplant implant removed on demand. The new focus of the family planning program has been on improving quality of care and ensuring couples greater freedom in their choice of contraceptive methods available both through the government and also through the private sector.[13]

Indonesia's National Family Planning Coordinating Board (BKKBN) issued a central-level policy change in 1992 (Hoesni, 2000). It involved an extensive series of training programs for field workers and service providers. New informational materials for providers and clients were developed, and a multifaceted service-based quality-improvement program was implemented. The extent to which field operations have actually been reformed based on the central-level policy remains a question, and the economic crisis of 1997 and 1998 no doubt interrupted the process. A recent recommendation called for a field assessment involving provincial and district-level managers, public and private service providers, field workers, and clients to determine if the policy change has become an operational reality (Hoesni, 2000).

Mexico. The Mexican government has had a national population policy to reduce population growth and fertility since 1973. Several

---

[13]During the mid-1980s, the Indonesian government began to promote the development of private commercial markets for family planning services and products (e.g., the Blue Circle campaign). This effort was in response to reduced public funding for family planning due to an economic downturn and thus seen as a strategy to encourage contraceptive users who could afford to, to start paying for services from the private sector.

public health institutions carry out the family planning program.[14] When the effort to promote use of contraception in rural areas was launched in 1977, the government set monthly targets for new contraceptive acceptors for hospitals and clinics to meet. These targets were to "motivate doctors, nurses, community health workers, and traditional births attendants to recruit new acceptors" among the rural population (Potter, 1999, p. 717). "The Mexican program fostered an interventionist style on the part of the personnel (medical personnel) who were charged with putting it into practice" (Potter, 1999, p. 718). In one of the three public health institutions, method-specific targets were set, giving high priority to IUDs and sterilization. The medical personnel at this institution were well trained about the nature of the reproductive risks faced by women in childbearing. Consequently, these providers held common views on how many children women should have, on how births should be spaced, and that the IUD and sterilization were the providers' favored methods. The attitude of the health personnel was very paternalistic in that they believed they knew best what women needed. There was a strong emphasis on providing IUDs and sterilization to women immediately after delivery (postpartum). Because decisions about accepting an IUD were often made very close to the time it was provided, the government's official norms assuring informed consent[15] by the woman were not always followed (Potter, 1999; Center for Reproductive Law and Policy and Grupo de Información en Reproducción Elegida, 1997).

---

[14]The three public health institutions that provide family planning services in Mexico are Instituto Mexicano de Seguro Social (IMSS, the Mexican Social Security Institute), which has both urban and rural programs; Secretaría de Salud (the Mexican Ministry of Health); and Instituto de Seguridad y Servicios Sociales de los Trabajadores del Estado (the Social Security Institute for State Workers), which provides services to government employees and teachers, as opposed to the regular employed population, which is served by IMSS.

[15]Informed consent is the communication between client and provider that confirms that the client has made a voluntary choice to use or receive a medical method or procedure. Health care providers are often required by law or institutional policies to obtain informed consent in writing before the administration of certain procedures (Association for Voluntary Surgical Contraception, 2000). In Mexico, revised norms for family planning service delivery were developed by an interinstitutional committee comprised of public and private institutions involved in the provision of reproductive health services, including family planning NGOs and women's groups (Seltzer, Lassner, and Yamashita, 1997).

The government launched a major training effort in the late 1990s that focused on counseling and informed consent at all three public health institutions. The effort was undertaken in response to government agencies' recognition that the informed consent process needed to be improved and also in response to a report by women's NGOs in Mexico and the United States of instances in which informed consent procedures for IUD insertion and sterilization were not followed (Seltzer, Lassner, and Yamashita, 1997; Center for Reproductive Law and Policy and Grupo de Informacion en Reproducción Elegida, 1997). In addition to the training efforts, a related mass media campaign was conducted to educate women and couples about "informed demand" so that they would have the knowledge and be able to exercise their rights in deciding what services they needed and would request. Both of these efforts were supported by the Government of Mexico and USAID. Given that the Mexican public health institutions are large bureaucracies that have been providing services for many years, it will no doubt take additional and sustained effort to ensure that significant quality improvements are achieved (USAID/Mexico, 2000; Beamish, Palma, and Seltzer, 2001).

Peru. In 1997, problems surfaced with the Government of Peru's strategy to make surgical contraception more available. In carrying out sterilization campaigns, Ministry of Health workers interpreted government planning figures as production targets, which led to instances where women felt pressured to undergo sterilization (Latin American and Caribbean Committee for the Defense of Women's Rights and the Center for Reproductive Law and Policy, 1999). A Tripartite Commission was established in 1997 to investigate the allegations of insufficient counseling prior to voluntary sterilization procedures. The Commission's review concluded that the criticism was exaggerated, but that the quality of services needed to be improved (UNFPA, 1999a). The government initiated a major reform effort in 1998. A USAID-funded project, the Coverage with Quality Project, has been a prime vehicle for various reform activities including training of providers in counseling. In addition, the Government of Peru's Ombudsman's Office and the Peruvian Colegio Médico (medical association) have been advising the Ministry of Health and investigating complaints against the government program (USAID, 1999a).

Advocating for Human Rights in Family Planning Programs

The examples described above illustrate how a number of family planning programs pursued practices that were contrary to the basic principles of voluntarism. In these instances, national goals and objectives were carried out for societal or collective benefits in such a way that individual rights and welfare were sometimes compromised. In part because of the vigilance of the local media and women's groups, in part because of the influence of international donors, and in part through candid admissions by governments, concerted efforts have been undertaken to address these problems.

One example from the United States is relevant to this point. Partly in response to human rights violations in Peru, the U.S. Congress adopted legislation in 1998, referred to as the Tiahrt amendment, which placed renewed emphasis on USAID's long-standing commitment to the principles of voluntarism and informed choice in family planning and opposition to coercive sterilization and abortion or to the promotion or performance of abortion. The amendment established several new requirements on family planning projects and, among other provisions, prohibited the use of quotas for numbers of births, family planning acceptors, and acceptors of a particular method as well as incentives to individuals for becoming acceptors or to program personnel for achieving targets or quotas (USAID, 1999b).

The relationship between governments and donors in implementing family planning programs is complex. Many developing countries were encouraged and assisted by donors to adopt policies to reduce population growth and fertility. In the implementation of the very programs designed to achieve those policies, various practices were pursued that were subsequently found to be unacceptable. Intrusive government actions appeared to have ignored the voluntaristic and individual welfare assumptions of family planning programs (McNicoll, 1997). While governments have sovereign rights in determining their domestic policies and programs, international donors have a responsibility to influence those programs to respect basic human rights and welfare. Whether or not one agrees with the demographic or societal rationale for population policies and family planning programs, the attention now given to human rights will help counter the tendency of some governments to ignore those rights (Mason, 1996). In this context, the ICPD Program of Action gave an important message to governments and international donors and a needed correction to the implementation of family planning programs.

Chapter Four

HEALTH RATIONALE

This chapter discusses several aspects of the health rationale for family planning programs. First is the role of contraceptive technology and concerns about contraceptive safety. Second is the health benefits of regulating fertility. Third is the relationship between abortion and family planning. Fourth is the concern over the quality of care in family planning programs. The final aspect is the broader context of reproductive health for family planning services.

CONTRACEPTIVE TECHNOLOGY

The appropriate role of contraceptive technology has been a key element of the controversy over family planning programs.[1] Critics of family planning programs and contraceptive technology questioned whether they would be the technological fix that proponents assumed, and many raised health concerns about contraceptive technology.

In the late 1960s and 1970s, the emerging women's health movement in the United States also took issue with the emphasis on contraceptive technology. Subsequently, a growing international network of women's health advocates questioned the process by which contraceptives were selected and introduced in developing countries. The perspective of women's health advocates on contraceptive

---

[1]Chapter Three addresses another aspect of this controversy in terms of the appropriate role of family planning programs as a public policy for addressing high fertility and population growth.

technology reflected fundamental differences with that of scientists who have been in the forefront of contraceptive development and introduction. The two views were articulated at a 1991 meeting of women's health advocates and scientists, and have been succinctly characterized as the "hardware" versus the "software" enthusiasts (WHO, 1991, p. 10). The view of scientists, the "hardware" enthusiasts, was that fertility regulation can be greatly enhanced through the development of a wider range of effective, safe, and acceptable methods; a basic concern of theirs was testing the safety and effectiveness of new technologies. The view of women's health advocates, the "software" enthusiasts, placed great importance on the more qualitative context of women's lives and family planning programs rather than the technological or quantitative aspects of contraception. These advocates sought to understand the needs of women and providers and the social and cultural influences of women's lives and the ability of women to take advantage of contraception. Furthermore, they considered it important to assess the characteristics of service delivery systems and the conditions in which methods would be used in order to determine how contraceptive technologies should be selected and introduced in different settings. The women's health advocates held that the safety and efficacy of contraceptive methods were significantly affected by the infrastructure of health and family planning programs.

The following two examples of the introduction of contraceptive technology confirm concerns of women's health advocates. In one case, a nonsurgical sterilization method, quinacrine pellets, has been used in a number of developing countries that ignore internationally accepted standards for testing experimental methods of new contraception for their safety and efficacy. No drug regulatory organization in the world, including the U.S. FDA, has approved quinacrine. International experts, including those from WHO and the FDA, and women's health advocates have called for a halt to its use until the necessary toxicological testing of quinacrine in animals and proper clinic trials are done (Berer, 1994, 1995). Quinacrine is an exceptional case in the history of the introduction of new contraceptives because of the disregard for international standards for testing new methods by some individuals who promoted the method and by some developing countries that provided the method.

The introduction of Norplant, an implant placed under the skin of a woman's upper arm, is quite a different story. After decades of careful development and testing, following well-defined standards for expert scientific review and consensus on safety and efficacy prior, Norplant is now used in many countries around the world including Indonesia, Thailand, and the United States (McCauley and Geller, 1992).[2] Even so, there have been problems with inadequate counseling of women about when the implant should be removed and inadequate training of providers for the management of side effects and removal of the implant. For example, "clinic staff providing Norplant do not always understand the meaning of menstrual blood in local cultures, and that frequent bleeding—a common side effect of Norplant—may result in the exclusion of women from sex, rituals or community life" (International Women's Health Coalition, 2000). An example from a proposed introduction of Norplant showed that careful assessment of the existing service delivery system might lead to a decision not to introduce a new method. In Vietnam, a joint assessment by the Vietnam Ministry of Health, the Vietnam Women's Union, the UNFPA, and WHO concluded that the added burdens on the service delivery system were sufficient that the introduction of a new contraceptive such as Norplant might actually reduce rather than improve the quality of care (Hieu, 1995; Finger and Keller, 1995).

The issue of contraceptive safety has been of particular concern to women's health advocates as the potential role of contraceptive technology has been considered. Some methods of contraception (such as the early formulations of the pill with its high level of estrogen) carried health risks for women. Improvements have been made in the safety, efficacy, and acceptability of many methods, but issues of safety remain since some methods continue to have health risks and are not recommended for users with particular characteristics or health conditions. For example, women ages 35 and over who are heavy smokers (over 20 cigarettes a day) should not take combined

---

[2]The USAID population assistance program only funds those contraceptive methods that have been approved by the U.S. FDA for use in the United States. Thus, for example, USAID did not fund the provision of the injectable, Depo Provera, for many years until the FDA finally approved the method in 1992.

oral contraceptive (COC) pills[3] because of the increased risk of stroke and heart attack from estrogen. Similarly, women with high blood pressure also should not take COCs (Hatcher et al., 1997). One response to the issue of contraceptive safety on the part of family planning programs and medical professionals was to weigh the risks of contraception against those of pregnancy, childbirth, and unsafe, usually illegal, abortion in developing countries. In this analysis, the health benefits of contraception outweigh the risks, although risks of particular methods for particular women are clearly identified and acknowledged (NAS, 1989). In addition, there are health benefits associated with some contraceptive methods, such as a reduced incidence of endometrial cancer for women who take the pill, that far outweigh the risks (Winikoff and Sullivan, 1987; NAS, 1989).

Women's health advocates have not found the relative risk assessment of contraception and pregnancy explanation satisfactory (Hartman, 1987; Dixon-Mueller, 1993). They favor comparing the risks of different contraceptives; making sure that women know all the safety issues and health risks, not just the risk of dying associated with given methods; and ensuring that women make their own decisions about what method to use based on full knowledge. In their view, contraceptive safety should be defined in different terms. Priority should be given to (1) methods with few side effects, (2) methods that also protect against STDs, and (3) methods that are controlled by the user (WHO, 1991). As has been noted in the discussion of the supply of family planning services, a wider range of simpler and safer methods are generally available, but women's health advocates wanted more attention given to less-used methods that have few if any side effects and are controlled by women, such as the diaphragm, and to condoms that protect against STDs.

Differences among women's health advocates and those supporting and developing contraceptive technology have been articulated thanks in part to the 1991 WHO meeting on fertility regulation technologies. At that time, there was a wide divide between these different perspectives, but optimism that "common ground" could be established and pursued through a series of recommendations that

---

[3]COC pills contain two hormones: estrogen and progestin.

called for greater involvement of women's health advocates and taking into account women's perspectives as research needs and priorities are determined and as research is carried out. Since that original meeting, WHO's Human Reproductive Programme has sponsored a series of Creating Common Ground meetings and has sponsored research on barrier methods (e.g., diaphragm) and on the informed consent process[4] in contraceptive research. It has developed a programming guide on the female condom for governments and NGOs interested in introducing the method. It has also supported a training initiative on gender and reproductive health for health program managers and planners in developing countries (Cottingham, Bergin, and Hilber, 1999).

HEALTH BENEFITS OF REGULATING FERTILITY

Improved maternal and child health has long been an expected benefit of family planning programs. The contribution of family planning to maternal and child survival in developing countries was increasingly documented through research studies published in the 1980s (Maine, 1981; Winikoff and Sullivan, 1987; NAS, 1989). The research results confirmed that family planning, or women's use of safe and effective contraception, helps to reduce maternal mortality by reducing the number of births and high-risk pregnancies. An NAS study concluded, "maternal mortality may be reduced by:

- Reducing the total number of pregnancies each woman has;

- Reducing the number of high-order births (5th order or higher);

- Reducing the number of births to very young women (aged 17 and younger) and to older women (over age 35);

---

[4]"Although guidelines exist for research on human subjects, these guidelines are often not followed completely or meaningful at either national or clinic levels" (WHO, 1991, p. 27). WHO's research in this area is designed to understand the actual process of informed consent in developing countries and to improve practices.

- Reducing the use of abortion to end unwanted pregnancies; and

- Reducing the number of pregnancies to women with major health problems." (NAS, 1989, p. 2.)

Similarly, the research showed that spacing between births, maternal age, and birth order were associated with child health and survival. Family planning had the potential to improve child health and survival by reducing the number of births associated with higher risks. "Infant and child mortality may be reduced by:

- Reducing the number of births that occur within approximately two years of a previous birth;

- Reducing the number of children born to very young mothers (those under 15 years of age);

- Reducing the number of children born to women in poor health; and

- Reducing the number of high-order births"(especially the 5th or higher-order births)" (NAS, 1989, p. 2).

Partly because of the research on the health benefits of family planning, the health rationale for family planning programs became more prominent during the 1980s. This was also a decade in which there was increased international concern with maternal and child survival. For example, UNICEF adopted its health intervention strategy in the mid-1980s that included a number of key interventions to improve child survival, one of which was family planning (Grant, 1990).[5] The World Bank spearheaded the Safe Motherhood initiative, beginning with an international conference on safe motherhood in Nairobi, Kenya in 1987. UNFPA also included among its rationales for family planning "improvements in family health" (Sadik, 1990).

---

[5]The strategy was referred to as GOBI-FFF and included growth monitoring (G), oral rehydration therapy (O), breastfeeding and better weaning practices (B), immunizations (I), food supplementation (F), family (child) spacing (F), and promotion of female literacy and the enhancement of the role of women (F).

Population organizations also gave greater emphasis to the health rationale for family planning programs (Rinehart and Kols, 1984; Population Reference Bureau, 1986).

The conservative domestic political climate in the United States in the early 1980s prompted USAID to develop a policy paper that presented a summary and objectives for its population assistance program (USAID, 1982). The paper underscored the importance of support for voluntary population and family planning programs in the agency's overall development assistance. The objectives for the U.S. population assistance program were based not only on humanitarian and strategic interests but also addressed issues of rights and welfare. The objectives of the program were to "(1) enhance the freedom of individuals in LDCs [less-developed countries] to choose voluntarily the number and spacing of their children, and (2) to encourage population growth consistent with the growth of economic resources and productivity" (USAID, 1982, p. 4).[6] The USAID policy stated that family planning assistance "provides critically important health benefits for mothers and young children" (USAID, 1982, p. 1).[7] However, it was not until several years later and in part prompted by research findings on the health consequences of contraception and reproduction that USAID added an explicit health rationale for its population assistance: "to improve the health and survival of mothers and children by promoting adequate birth spacing; encouraging childbearing during the safest years for women; and by reducing abortions" resulting from unwanted pregnancies (Gillespie, 1987).

The health rationale was also an important part of population policy considerations in Africa. Through the 1970s, African countries had not viewed population growth as a major factor in their development strategies given the small size of most of the populations (34 of 48 African countries had populations under 5 million in 1978). Not until the mid-1980s did concern about rapid population growth in the region begin to find public expression (Chamie, 1994). But even then,

---

[6]This paper described the basic principles and policies governing U.S. population assistance, including voluntarism and informed choice as well as prohibitions on support for promotion of abortion or for actual services (1974 legislation) and for involuntary sterilization (1978 legislation).

[7]A director of USAID's Office of Population during the 1980s stated that the health rationale was always part of the Agency's population assistance program (Speidel, 2000).

African governments and international donors found the health rationale a compelling reason to promote family planning programs. Birth spacing had been part of traditional practices in African countries and was achieved through long postpartum sexual abstinence and breast-feeding. There was evidence that the durations of postpartum abstinence and breast-feeding were decreasing (Caldwell and Caldwell, 1987; Caldwell, Orubuloye, and Caldwell, 1992). Family planning was an effective means to achieve birth spacing.

ABORTION AND FAMILY PLANNING

The controversy over abortion has influenced family planning programs and also had implication for women's health. To appreciate how the controversy has affected family programs, some background on the relationship between family planning programs and abortion is helpful.

From the earliest days of family planning programs, prevention of abortion to reduce related maternal mortality and morbidity has been an important part of the health rationale for promoting contraception. In Latin American countries in the 1960s, where abortion was illegal, there were serious public health concerns about the large number of hospitalizations related to abortion complications. Today, preventing abortion continues to be an important reason to support and promote family planning in all world regions. Historical examples from different countries show that, over the long run, increasing use of contraception is associated with reductions in abortion. This has been true for diverse countries including Chile, Japan, South Korea, and those that were formerly part of the Soviet Union in Central and Eastern Europe and Central Asia (Salter, Johnston, and Hengren, 1997; Westoff et al., 1998). Recent data from Bangladesh show that higher use of contraception is associated with a lower incidence of abortion (Rahman, DaVanzo, and Razzaque, 2001; see also p. 120 in this report). There is still a large number of abortions in some countries, including ones that have high prevalence of contraception such as China, Japan, and the United States (Freedman and

Freedman, 1992). For example, there were over 1.3 million abortions in the United States in 1996 (Henshaw, 1998). [8]

The relationship between abortion and family planning programs is not just a matter of women's health. It has ethical and legal dimensions that have caused abortion to be one of the most divisive issues in the population field. Vehement opposition to abortion is based on religious and ethical values that define it as morally unacceptable. Opponents of abortion include the Catholic Church, religious fundamentalists, some Islamic groups, and right-to-life groups (many of which are Catholic or fundamentalist). Supporters of access to safe, legal services for voluntary pregnancy termination hold that it is a basic right of women both in terms of the personal *freedom* for a woman to control her body and for individuals and couples to determine the number and spacing of children. Some go on to say that abortion should be considered a social *entitlement*, just as family planning is, in that individuals and couples are entitled to the information and the means to control their fertility safely and effectively; for these abortion-rights advocates, abortion is one means of fertility control (Dixon-Mueller, 1993). Supporters of the right to abortion include many medical and family planning associations, women's organizations, and public health officials.

The grounds on which abortion is permitted vary among countries and cover a range from the most restrictive, "to save the woman's life," to the most liberal, "allowing abortion on request." The vast majority of countries in the world (173 of 179) permit abortion in order to save the woman's life, but only 36 countries permit abortion on request (United Nations, 1998). Even where abortion is legal, there is no assurance that women have access to safe services. There are many reasons for limited access, including shortages of facilities, equipment, and trained providers; programmatic restrictions; and reluctance or refusal of some health professionals to perform abortions (Dixon-Mueller, 1993).

---

[8]For additional information on the effects of family planning on abortion, see DaVanzo and Grammich (forthcoming).

The lack of access coupled with the restrictive or illegal status of abortion in many countries means that there continues to be a large number of abortions performed under unsafe circumstances. Of an estimated 50 million induced abortions worldwide per year, it is estimated that 20 million abortions are performed under unsafe circumstances or by untrained providers. Additionally, there are an estimated 70,000 deaths each year that are a consequence of unsafe abortion, and nearly all of these occurred in developing countries (Tsui, Wasserheit, and Haaga, 1997). It is apparent that many women resort to abortion regardless of its legal status and risk health complications and even death in doing so. Reducing the number of abortions, particularly unsafe abortions, is a public health goal in many developing countries.

The controversy over abortion has affected family planning programs in at least three ways. First, there is a split among those who see abortion as a method of family planning and those who see it as a service quite apart from family planning. Second, the controversy over abortion has affected funding levels for population assistance and use of funds from certain donors. Third, there is growing recognition of the critical need and opportunities for postabortion care in reproductive health and family planning programs as a way to reduce subsequent abortion.

Whether abortion is considered a means of family planning is influenced by the political debate. For example, donors, such as USAID and UNFPA, state that abortion is not a means of family planning since the practice of contraception involves a proactive step of preventing pregnancy in the first place. Abortion is fertility regulation, but not family planning. Feminists and women's health advocates see abortion as a basic right for women's health and as an essential means of fertility regulation within the broader scope of reproductive health and family planning services. For these abortion-rights advocates, abortion is necessary not only as a backup to contraceptive failure, but also because of the large unmet need for contraception, it may be a woman's only alternative for not having an unintended birth. The American public is also unsure about whether the term *family planning* includes abortion, based on the results of a 1998 public opinion survey (Adamson et al., 2000). Regardless of whether the definition of family planning includes abortion or not, many women do resort to unsafe, clandestine abortion since most family planning programs—particularly those that receive some external donor funding—do not provide abortion services.

The controversy over abortion has also affected donor funding of family planning programs in developing countries. There is a group of conservatives and right-to-lifers in the United States that is opposed not only to abortion but to artificial contraception and sterilization. This group has brought pressure on the legislative process in the United States, and the group's efforts appear to have been successful in reducing the level of funding for U.S. population assistance in recent years. In addition, these conservative elements have influenced how those funds could be spent. First announced by President Reagan following the 1984 UN Population Conference, the so-called "Mexico City policy" (sometimes called the "Global Gag Rule") was adopted by the U.S. government; the policy prohibited USAID from supporting NGOs that used their own funds to promote or support abortions. While the newly elected Clinton administration lifted this restriction in 1993, Congress attached a similar restriction to population assistance for 2000.[9] Many have observed that this funding restriction would be deemed unconstitutional if applied to U.S. organizations working in the United States, not only because abortion is a constitutional right, but also because of freedom of speech. Among his first acts in office, President George W. Bush reinstated the Mexico City policy in January 2001.

There is growing interest among donors, assistance organizations in population and health, and developing countries in promoting postabortion services to women as a program strategy for reducing future unintended pregnancies, abortions, and especially unsafe abortions. Few clinics and hospitals that treat women suffering from abortion complications offer contraceptive counseling and services as part of their postabortion care (Salter, Johnston, and Hengren, 1997). Provision of postabortion care that includes family planning apparently presents no legal and funding restrictions, even where abortion is illegal, since the intention is preventing future abortions. There is a growing literature on the delivery of postabortion care that

---

[9]A cap of $15 million was set on funding to foreign NGOs and multilateral organizations that are unwilling to certify that they will not perform legal abortions or advocate for changes in existing abortion laws, even if they use their own funds for such activities (Population Action International, 2000).

provides useful examples of program experience in many developing countries (Huntington et al., 1995; Salter, Johnston, and Hengren, 1997; Population Council, 1998a, 1998b; Mundigo and Indriso, 1999; Pathfinder International, 1999).

Despite the rising use of contraception worldwide, current evidence suggests that there will continue to be unintended pregnancies (either from contraceptive failure or not using contraception) and women who will choose to end those pregnancies through abortion, whether legal or illegal. Given this reality, the future challenge for family planning and reproductive health programs is to redouble efforts to satisfy the unmet need for contraception. Where abortion is legal, health programs need to ensure adequate access to medically safe, effective abortion. Whether abortion is legal or not, programs need to ensure adequate access to postabortion care that includes contraceptive counseling and services.

QUALITY OF CARE IN FAMILY PLANNING PROGRAMS

Quality of care has been a major issue for improving the delivery of contraceptive services for more than a decade. This is not to say that quality of services was not important prior to this (Jain, 1989). Program administrators have long been aware that "satisfied users" help to spread the word to other potential clients. Increased concern about quality of care was not a controversial topic for family planning programs as much as it was a criticism of the relative importance given to certain aspects of service delivery programs by some donors, developing countries, and those evaluating programs.

Interest in the quality of care of programs was raised in the past decade for several reasons. Feminists and women's health advocates called for more attention to clients' health, needs, and rights (based on the rights of individuals and couples to achieve their reproductive goals) and individual welfare partly to counter the emphasis on national goals for population control (see discussion in Chapter Three). Demographers and analysts of family planning programs urged that improving the quality of care should help to satisfy individuals' and couples' needs for fertility control and enable them to achieve their reproductive intentions or goals. Analysts also hypothesized that "improvements in the quality of services will result in a larger, more committed clientele of satisfied contraceptive users. Over the long run, a more committed clientele of satisfied individuals will translate into higher contraceptive prevalence, and ultimately, reduction in fertility" (Jain, Bruce, and Kumar, 1992, p. 213). Thus, greater attention to quality of care should, in theory, help meet individual needs for fertility control and societal goals of fertility reduction.

There was evidence from some family planning programs suggesting that an overemphasis on access to contraception was detracting from other more qualitative aspects of service delivery and thus the programs were not adequately meeting clients' needs and promoting their health and welfare (Bruce, 1990). Access was defined by whether services were available (i.e., proximate to clients in terms of distance, travel time, ease, and cost of travel) and were affordable to potential users. Furthermore, it was thought that judging success of service delivery through quantitative measures, such as number of acceptors or number of contraceptives distributed, ignored more qualitative aspects such as whether clients were satisfied with the services and how well services helped clients to meet their reproductive needs.

Some of the evidence for a lack of attention to quality of care is based on the existence of two different groups: (a) users of contraception who for various reasons discontinued use and (b) individuals and couples with an unmet need for family planning. By addressing the needs of these two groups, more couples would be able to achieve their reproductive goals.

Discontinuation of use of a particular method of contraception is common and may be an indication that individuals' and couples' needs are not being met. Data on rates of discontinuation from a number of countries show a wide range—from a low of 20 percent in Zimbabwe to a high of 65 percent in the Dominican Republic of women who stop using a method of contraception (i.e., any method except sterilization) within a year of starting (Table 4.1) (Curtis and Blanc, 1997). There are several reasons why women may stop using a particular method. Some women stop using a method because they no longer need to use it (e.g., they want to get pregnant or their risk of pregnancy is less[10]). Others stop using a method because their partner forbids continued use. Yet others stop using a method because they have health concerns or suffer undesirable side effects. For example, more than 60 percent of women who discontinued a method of contraception in Bangladesh did so because of side effects or for other method-related reasons (Curtis and Blanc, 1997). Method failure is another reason for discontinuation. In both Peru and the Philippines, contraceptive failure was the most important reason that women stopped using a method; this reflected the high prevalence of traditional methods in those populations (Curtis and Blanc, 1997). In addition, clients may stop using a method if they do not get their preferred choice or if they are treated rudely by providers (Kols and Sherman, 1998).

Even though discontinuing use of a particular contraceptive method is not unusual, some of those who stop using one method switch to another method. Research on discontinuation suggests that studying the contraceptive history of women or couples gives a more useful picture of their experience than only looking at discontinued use of a given method. This broader view is especially important since switching methods can help couples meet their changing reproductive needs over time (Jain, 1989).[11] A classic analysis of the contraceptive status of IUD recipients was based on data from Taiwan. Thirty months after a group of women had first accepted an IUD, only 28 percent were still using the original IUD, although a total of 47 percent of these women were using an IUD given that some had had another IUD inserted, and another 26 percent were using other methods of contraception; thus, 73 percent of the original IUD acceptors were current contraceptive users (Freedman and Takeshita, 1969, cited in Jain, 1989). More recent evidence of discontinuation showed that in Bangladesh, of the 50 percent of users who discontinued use after 12 months, 15 percent had no need for contraception,

---

[10]Exposure to the risk of pregnancy may change as women age and become less fecund, if women become divorced or widowed, or if their husband is away for a significant period of time.

[11]The picture is even more complicated since rates of discontinuation vary by method (Jain, 1989). In addition, method choice is influenced by women's weighing various factors, such as the ease of use and the risk of failure for a given method (Curtis and Blanc, 1997).

Table 4.1

Contraceptive Discontinuation for All Methods Except Sterilization
(percent of users discontinuing during their first year of use)

Country	Survey Year	Percent
Bangladesh	1993/94	49.4
Brazil (NE)	1991	59.6
Colombia	1990	45.2
Dominican Republic	1991	64.9
Egypt	1995	30.5
Indonesia	1997	23.8
Paraguay	1990	59.1
Peru	1991/92	48.9
Philippines	1993	37.2
Turkey	1993	37.1
Zimbabwe	1994	19.7

SOURCES: Curtis and Blanc (1997); Mahran, El-Zanaty, and Way (1998) (Egypt); Fathonah (2000) (Indonesia).

20 percent had switched to another method, and 15 percent had abandoned contraceptive use although they still had a need (Table 2.3 in Curtis and Blanc, 1997).

Reasons for discontinuation may reflect differing motivations among users to control their fertility and may also reflect characteristics of service delivery systems. The motivation of couples to control their fertility varies; those with weaker motivations may more easily abandon contraception.[12]

---

[12]In most settings, increases in the desire to limit family size contribute far more to trends in contraceptive use and fertility decline than do increases in the desire to space births (Bongaarts, 1992). In sub-Saharan Africa, however, contraceptive use for spacing of births has been substantial and more important for trends in contraceptive use than the desire to limit family size (Caldwell, Orubuloye, and Caldwell, 1992). In a study of contraceptive discontinuation in six high-prevalence countries (Indonesia, Thailand, Egypt, Morocco, Tunisia, and Ecuador), the strength of motivation (i.e., those more motivated to use a method more carefully) was important for method failure in that younger women who had not reached their desired family size had higher rates of failure than older women, who had generally already reached or exceeded their preferred number of children (Ali and Cleland, 1995).

Some reasons for discontinuation may indicate poor quality of care in the service delivery program.[13] For example, counseling may not be adequate to determine clients' reproductive needs, their desired choice of method, and their concerns about side effects. Providers may have inadequate technical knowledge and competence. There may be power, class, or language differences between service providers and clients that cause clients to be reluctant to ask questions or return for follow-up counseling. Further, the harsh bureaucratic culture in some settings may be off-putting to clients (Simmons, 2000). The stock of contraceptive supplies, such as a particular brand of oral contraceptives or injectables, may be uncertain. Many of these factors are components of quality of care of service delivery.

The second group for whom the lack of quality of services may be important is those individuals and couples with an unmet need for family planning. Programs have been criticized for not giving enough attention to understanding why these individuals and couples, with an apparent need to practice contraception, are not doing so. The most common reasons given for not using contraception among women with an unmet need (based on both survey data and anthropological research) are lack of knowledge, fear of side effects, and social and familial (especially husband's) disapproval (Bongaarts and Bruce, 1995). These reasons reflect inadequate quality of services as well as underlying sociocultural influences and suggest that programmatic and cultural issues are intertwined. For example, lack of knowledge and fear of side effects can be addressed by better training of providers and better counseling of clients. Social opposition to contraception can also be addressed by programs, but is related to underlying social and cultural values that are more difficult to change and that, in any case, presumably change more slowly.

Given the many issues about quality of care as a key aspect of improving the delivery of services, a framework was developed that has guided both the understanding of quality of care among analysts and critics of family planning programs and subsequent research for over

---

[13]Problems of availability and costs of methods were not usually given as reasons for discontinuation in a six-country study of contraceptive discontinuation (Ali and Cleland, 1995).

a decade. The quality-of-care framework has six components (Bruce, 1990):

- choice of methods
- information given to clients
- technical competence of service providers

- interpersonal relations between clients and providers
- follow-up services for continuing care
- constellation of related health services

Only one of these, choice of methods, will be examined here as an example to show how clients' choice of methods has been limited and that certain practices in the provision of particular methods reflect poor service quality and may have compromised clients' health, needs, and welfare.[14]

Method Choice

One of the central characteristics of good quality of care is having an adequate range of methods available to meet the need of users. Method choice is considered important because clients have a right to choose which contraceptive method is best for them.[15] Users also have different reproductive needs: some want to space births and need temporary methods such as pills or injectables; some want to

---

[14]For additional information on the various dimensions of quality of care in family planning programs, see Bertrand, Hardee, Magnani, and Angle (1995); Koenig, Hossain, and Whittaker (1997); Tsui, Wasserheit, and Haaga (1997, pp. 103–106); Kols and Sherman (1998); Barnett and Stein (1998); and Koenig, Foo, and Joshi (2000). Looking at only one component of quality of care can be misleading since various aspects are interrelated. For example, research in rural Bangladesh suggested that it was "not the absolute number of methods offered to the client, but rather the degree of trust, rapport, and confidence established between the field worker and the client" that was most important in the relationship between method choice and acceptance (Simmons and Elias, 1994, p. 3, cited in Koenig, Hossain, and Whittaker, 1992).

[15]Among the rights in the IPPF Chart of Sexual and Reproductive Rights is the "Right to Health Care and Health Protection." Included under this right is that "Every person has the right to sexual and reproductive health care including the right of choice to decide whether to use services, and which contraception method" (IPPF, 1996, p. 22).

limit births and may need longer-term methods such as IUDs or sterilization; and some are at risk of both pregnancy and STDs and need a method that protects them against both risks, such as condoms. Users also have different health risks and tolerance for side effects associated with particular methods. Furthermore, the needs of contraceptive users can change over time. Finally, method choice is also important for client satisfaction and continued use since giving clients their preferred method is associated with more sustained use (Pariani, Heer, and Arsdol, 1991). Programs that encourage switching of methods can help prevent dropouts and enhance user satisfaction. In defining how choice of contraceptive methods should be considered, Jain suggested that

> In principle, a program should offer enough methods to competently service significant subgroups (e.g., spacers, limiters, males/females . . . and so forth). The issues here are to arrive at a minimum and optimum number of methods that a program should offer, and to develop management capabilities that will assist users in switching easily among available methods (Jain, 1989, p. 2).

In addition to meeting users' needs and increasing user satisfaction, availability of a wider range of contraceptive methods can also mean higher overall levels of contraceptive prevalence. For example, an expanded choice of contraceptive methods increased overall prevalence of contraceptive use between 1965 and 1973 at the national level in Hong Kong, India, South Korea, Taiwan, and Thailand and between 1977 and 1981 for the Matlab and Maternal-Child Health/Family Planning Extension projects in Bangladesh (Jain, 1989, pp. 6–7).

Despite the wide availability of modern contraception throughout the world and a range of contraceptive methods with varying characteristics, there are numerous examples of limitations on method choice. Among a group of 26 countries, contraceptive use is concentrated on one or two methods in many countries, and this concentration shows "how little use is made in so many places of contraceptive technology that is actually available today" (Potter, 1999, p. 705). Why this concentration exists appears rooted in women's inclination to stay with a method, in the biases of service delivery providers and programs, and in the tendency of providers to recommend particular methods and of clients to accept such recommendations (Potter, 1999).

Assessing the degree to which contraceptive method choice exists in family planning programs entails looking at whether there is choice for significant groups of users,[16] and whether there are biases and restrictions in programs. Provider biases have been confirmed in a number of countries in different regions. For example, private physicians in Jamaica and service providers in Tanzania and India clearly have such biases that may affect clients' choice of methods.

*   In Jamaica, the government's official service delivery guidelines state that the injectable Depo-Provera is a method for "women and adolescents who have at least one child." Among the private physicians who were interviewed in a study, however, the majority had never heard of, let alone used, the Jamaican government's guidelines. The physicians reported that, in their medical practice, only women who were over age 20 could use Depo-Provera. These physicians also reported that they would provide this method only to women who had had two children (Hardee et al., 1995).

*   In Tanzania, the Ministry of Health issued National Policy Guidelines and Standards for Family Planning in 1994 to establish uniform rights of access to all males and females of reproductive age, including adolescents. Even so, more than half of the doctors surveyed reported that they had age restrictions for pill use, while about 80 percent of trained midwives and health auxiliaries reported that they imposed such restrictions (Speizer et al., 2000).

*   In India, where sterilization is the predominant contraceptive method used, evidence from several states shows that service providers attached little importance to clients' preference for methods. One study, cited in a general review of quality of care in

---

[16]Jain, Bruce, and Kumar (1992) suggested assessing method choice by the following factors or characteristics: the total number of methods; temporary self-administered methods; methods suitable for sporadic use; permanent methods; methods with few or no side effects; methods for use by men; methods for use by women; methods that can be used without a partner's knowledge; methods suitable for adolescent, low-weight, malnourished, or breast-feeding women; and nonhormonal methods.

the Indian Family Welfare Programme, found that "93 percent of nurse/midwives interviewed in Karnataka stated that the provider decides which method the client should use" (Koenig, Foo, and Joshi, 2000, p. 4).

These examples show that it is not sufficient to issue service delivery guidelines, and that efforts must be undertaken to ensure that providers understand and follow the guidelines. Furthermore, evaluation of current practices is important to ensure that current practices conform to established guidelines and help to improve quality of care.

Programs emphasize certain methods (sterilization in India, IUDs and sterilization in Mexico) for various reasons. These include the cost and complexity of delivering a range of contraceptive methods and that methods, such as IUD and sterilization, are considered more effective methods for preventing pregnancy, and hence will help achieve demographic goals. Feminists and women's health advocates have criticized some programs for having too much emphasis on certain provider-dependent methods (IUDs, injectables, implants, and sterilization) in order to achieve given targets. The criticism is that such methods do not necessarily respond to women's health needs and rights and that the "overriding aim of family planning should become that of providing women with the means to achieve reproductive autonomy" (Smyth, 1991). These advocates hold that methods controlled by women, not providers, enhance women's autonomy.

To counter these criticisms, it has been suggested that many women prefer provider-controlled methods for various reasons. For example, some women like the privacy associated with using injectables, or a method that is independent of coitus such as the IUD, or the convenience of having a one-time procedure such as sterilization (e.g., in Catholic countries, some women view sterilization as a single act of sin, which can be forgiven; or in remote areas, resupply of a method like the pill may be difficult) (Crane, 2000).

A closely related issue raised by women's health advocates is that method choice has been affected by the medicalization of contraceptive services, which reduces users' or women's control over contraception. Women's health advocates were concerned that women had to depend on physicians and clinics for contraceptive services. These health advocates favored methods that not only had fewer health risks and side effects, but also would be controlled by women. An example of a woman-controlled method is the diaphragm. (WHO has supported research on user-controlled methods, see p. 97). Some of these methods have an important disadvantage in that they are generally less effective than other provider-dependent methods such as the IUD. Given that the methods advocated often carried higher risk of failure and thus greater risk of unintended pregnancy, women's health advocates have also favored access to safe, legal abortion. Abortion is not only seen as a backup to contraceptive failure, but as a basic right for women (Dixon-Mueller, 1993).

Women's health advocates have also criticized the emphasis on medically efficient, provider-dependent methods because not enough attention has been given to barrier methods, such as the condom, which can protect women against STDs and HIV infection. However, more and more countries around the world, in concert with the international donor community, are addressing prevention of STDs through use of condoms (Lande, 1993; Gardner, Blackburn, and Upadyay, 1999).

While provider and program biases can and do limit women's choices, there are other factors that can limit method choice. The cost of contraceptives or the lack of contraceptive supplies due to a weak logistics system may affect choice. Not only provider biases but also lack of provider competence about different methods and poor counseling may limit choice.

Women's health advocates have been concerned about harmful effects associated with poor quality programs and practices. Studies of practices in sterilization camps in India showed very inadequate counseling before and after the operation (Koenig, Koo, and Joshi, 2000). In addition, facilities were often inadequate, e.g., with unreliable sources of electricity and water, especially in outreach camps for sterilization (Koenig and Khan, 1999). This example, similar to that mentioned previously regarding Norplant, was evidence of a lack of attention to proper counseling of women and to adequate provider training and management.

Another example that dates back to the early 1970s represents health concerns about mode of delivery for certain contraceptive methods. During this period, a few programs, including Profamilia in Colombia, undertook efforts to expand access to family planning through CBD programs of pills and condoms. Despite initial misgivings about women's health risks associated with the provision of oral contraceptives through the CBD program, the practice became medically acceptable given the potential advantages of using oral contraception compared with the risks of childbirth or induced abortion (abortion was invariably performed illegally and thus posed even higher risks for women's health and survival). Research on the CBD programs has shown that the health risks were minimal and the acceptability of pills was high (Ross et al., 1987).

Health concerns about different contraceptive methods may be warranted in different settings. Oral contraceptives are typically available in many Latin American countries without prescription. In Brazil, where a high percentage of women smoke, many women used orals without prescription and without adequate screening for risk factors such as smoking and hypertension. It has been suggested that this may be a reason for high death rates from stroke among Brazilian women of reproductive age (DaVanzo and Haaga, 1991). In general, use of orals is not recommended for women ages 35 and over who smoke or suffer from hypertension. There have been counseling efforts in Brazil to encourage women smokers with cardiovascular problems to switch methods (Sociedad Civil Bem-Estar Familiar no Brasil, 1986). It is also possible that the sharp increase in sterilization among Brazilian women (from 17 to 40 percent between 1986 and 1996) is partly related to concerns about side effects from the pill (Potter, 1999; Merrick, 2000b).

Research on Quality of Care

Concerns over a lack of attention to quality of care in family planning programs have stimulated research aimed at improving the quality of care (including method choice) since the late 1980s. What has emerged from this research is a clearer understanding of the dimensions of quality of care and the characteristics of high-quality care, which in turn has led to some improvements in the quality of care delivered by family planning programs. The so-called Bruce framework provides the now standard definition of the elements of quality of care (see pp. 86–87 for the six elements in this framework). The framework is based on how individuals or clients are "treated by the system providing services" (Jain, 1989, p. 29). A high-quality program is defined as "one that is client oriented and aims to help individuals achieve their reproductive intentions or goals" (Jain, Bruce, and Mensch, 1992, p. 392).

Considerable effort has been devoted to developing indicators of quality of care and methods for evaluating quality. An interagency working group helped to develop lists of quality indicators for clinic-based, community-based, and social marketing programs (Bertrand, Magnani, and Knowles, 1994).[17] Working group participants agreed that there were three levels for measuring indicators of quality—management, providers, and clients—and that these levels were interrelated. Various data collection methods have been employed to obtain this range of information, and some of these are described below. Some of the research has pointed out the complexity and methodological difficulties of measuring different dimensions of quality of care and of developing indicators that are reliable and valid (Simmons and Elias, 1994; Léon, Quiroz, and Brazzoduro, 1994; Askew, Mensch, and Adewuyi, 1994).

For the most part, the discussion that follows deals broadly with quality-of-care issues rather than just the element of method choice. This is partly because efforts to assess and improve quality of care are often multifaceted.

Research has been conducted to determine the meaning of quality of care for women who receive reproductive health services and to measure service quality through client exit interviews and mystery clients[18] (Vera, 1993; Williams, Schutt-Aine, and Cuca, 2000; and Huntington and Schuler, 1993). "The simple act of asking the client her views, and obligating the service provider to listen to them, is

---

[17]A Service Delivery Working Group convened under the USAID-supported EVAL-UATION Project included representatives from numerous cooperating agencies in population.

[18]A mystery client is someone selected from the potential client population who poses as a participant or client in a program and who then reports on his or her experience to an evaluator of the program.

perhaps the most important outcome from [efforts to assess client satisfaction]" (Williams, Schutt-Aine, and Cuca, 2000, p. 70). Related research has pointed to the importance of educating not only providers, but also clients, about quality. Various studies have shown that clients, particularly those who are less educated or of lower status than the providers, do not have high expectations about the quality of services and are frequently satisfied with levels of care that would be considered substandard by Western standards (Koenig, Foo, and Joshi, 2000; Schuler and Hossain, 1998). Furthermore, cultural norms about appropriate client behavior during consultations may influence client behavior, suggesting that a strategy is needed that "raises clients' expectations and (at the same time) improves providers' communication and counseling skills" (Kim et al., 2000, p. 11).

Some programs have undertaken efforts to educate clients about their rights and choices. IPPF issued a set of 10 "rights of the client" to raise awareness of both clients and providers, and clinics of many IPPF affiliates exhibit a poster of these clients' rights. The National Population Council in Mexico conducted a media campaign designed to create more awareness of "informed demand" so that clients would be better informed about their reproductive needs and rights. This campaign was in addition to an extensive training program in counseling and informed consent for service providers at the three major public health institutions (Beamish, Palma, and Seltzer, 2001). In Egypt, the Gold Star Program, which involves an accrediting system based on 101 indicators of good quality, was designed not only to improve the quality of the government's family planning services but also to "create new expectations for quality so that the public will request better services" (El Gebaly et al., 1998, p. 20). The Egyptian Ministry of Health and Population and the Ministry of Information have worked together on this program since 1994 to improve and then monitor the quality of family planning units alongside a media campaign to increase client expectations.

A question that family planning specialists and researchers have increasingly tried to answer in recent years is whether quality of care really makes a difference in the delivery of family planning services. Are higher-quality programs better able to meet clients' needs? A group of five commissioned studies looked at the relationship between quality of care and the demand for family planning in

Brazil, Morocco, Tunisia, the Philippines, and Peru (Samara, Buckner, and Tsui, 1996). The results from this research provided strong evidence that quality matters. In one study in Peru, it was estimated that contraceptive practice would increase dramatically if high quality of services were provided. In the Philippines, among women who used modern/nonsurgical methods of contraception, several characteristics of the service provider setting (quality factors) increased use of public clinics. These factors included having a short distance to the clinic (0.6 kilometers), a variety of contraceptive methods, pre- and postnatal care and infant delivery services, and a physician on staff. Another study of the influence of quality of care in family planning services in rural Bangladesh found that quality made a difference in the decisions of women to adopt a contraceptive method and had an even greater effect on continued use of contraception (Koenig, Hossain, and Whittaker, 1997.)[19]

Comprehensive research on quality of care has been conducted in sub-Saharan Africa, Latin America, and Asia through an approach that assesses the strengths and limits of service delivery infrastructure as well as the quality of services (Miller et al., 1997; Mensch et al., 1994). The research has been used as a baseline against which to assess efforts to improve the quality of services. Additional research has been carried out that sheds light on aspects of quality of care although its purpose was to study women's experiences with family planning and to understand women's perspectives on the immediate and long-term consequences of family planning. For example, women's concerns with side effects of contraception—both real and perceived—were more serious than providers realized. Women saw side effects "as a critical factor in determining which methods they will use, whether they will continue a method, or whether they even start contraception" (Barnett and Stein, 1998, p. 48). This finding has important implications for the ways that providers counsel clients about their concerns and has led to improvements in provider training (Shane and Chalkley, 1998). One

---

[19]In this study, quality was measured by an index based on client responses to five questions about field-workers' care: (1) Is the field-worker responsive to your questions? (2) Is she appreciative of your need for privacy? (3) Is she someone you can depend on to help with your problems? (4) Is she sympathetic to your problems and needs? (5) When she explains something to you, does she provide enough information?

ongoing experimental study with the Ministry of Health (MOH) in Peru has found that the quality of client–provider interaction improved when providers used special interactive job aids during counseling sessions.[20] The MOH is interested in scaling up this intervention (León, 2001). Numerous other studies designed to improve quality of care in family planning and reproductive health programs have been supported under the USAID-funded FRONTIERS in Reproductive Health project (Population Council, 2000).

Men have an important role in decisions about contraceptive use in many settings, but they have tended to be marginalized by family planning programs and services. In the past several years, much more attention has been given to addressing the role of men in family planning and reproductive health (Helzner, 1996; Drennan, 1998; IPPF/WHR and AVSC, 1998; Pile et al., 1999; Cohen and Burger, 2000). This greater attention has been in part because of the added health risks to women and men of the AIDS epidemic and also because of a greater recognition that gender inequalities between women and men have a significant influence on women's health and well-being. Surveys of men have shown that many men "know and approve of family planning—in marked contrast to the stereotype of men as uncooperative or uninterested in family planning or reproductive health. . . but that most men need more family planning information, education, and services" (Drennan, 1998, p. 9). Recent research and program experience has also demonstrated that "many men care about and are willing to make positive contributions to the reproductive health of their partners and the well-being of their families" (Program for Appropriate Technology in Health, 2001, p. 1). Although various strategies have been tried to engage men as partners in improving women's reproductive health and to extend reproductive health services to men, most of the projects have been small in scale and have not provided information on how project activities have influenced relationships between women and men and gender equality.

---

[20]Interactive job aids are a set of cards (each card describes a contraceptive method) that a provider lays out on a desk in front of a client during a counseling session. Together, the provider and client discard the cards on methods that are not suitable to the client's needs, and they use the remaining cards to help the client select the most appropriate contraceptive method.

Efforts to improve quality by expanding contraceptive choice are often based on the introduction of a particular contraceptive that may be new in a given setting, such as Norplant or injectables. Spearheaded by WHO, a new approach to contraceptive introduction has been implemented in a number of countries (Spicehandler and Simmons, 1994; Simmons et al., 1997). It involves a participatory strategy involving government officials, service providers and administrators, and clients (users and nonusers of family planning) in assessing the overall service-delivery system and the range of available methods, and then implementing changes that are designed to improve the overall capacity of the service-delivery system. "This approach shifts attention from an exclusive emphasis on new technology to a holistic view of factors relevant for method introduction, including a concern for the social context of method choice, the currently available method mix, and the organizational capacity of the program to ensure quality of care" (Diaz et al., 1999, p. 1). Such a "participatory action research project" was implemented in a municipality in southern Brazil and led to improved reproductive options, not just in family planning, but also in other reproductive health services, including prenatal care. A participatory approach to introducing new contraceptives helps to counter the criticism of contraception as a technological fix.

The emphasis on method choice and clients' rights may have fostered research on client interest in a less-used method—the diaphragm—in part because it is under the user's control and has few side effects. For example, WHO supported an interagency collaborative study of the diaphragm in Colombia, the Philippines, and Turkey in the mid-1990s to assess its acceptability, service delivery requirements, and use-effectiveness (Ortayli et al., 2000).

Also in the interest of expanding method choice, there was increasing attention, beginning in the 1980s, given to the relationship between breast-feeding and fertility, and the role of breast-feeding for birth spacing. Subsequently, a number of studies were carried out, including a multicenter study in ten different populations in both developed and developing countries, to determine the acceptability, client satisfaction, effectiveness, and use of the lactational amenorrhea method (LAM). The results found that overall satisfaction with the method was high (84 percent) and that knowledge and understanding of the method was also high (ranging from 78 to 89 percent)

(Hight-Laukaran et al., 1997). Furthermore, the study found a high rate of effectiveness, 98.5 percent at six months postpartum, in a variety of cultural and socioeconomic settings when women carefully followed the criteria for using the method (Labbok et al., 1997). The authors concluded that LAM is acceptable and ready for widespread use and should be included in the range of services available in maternal and child health, family planning, and other primary health care settings (Hight-Laukaran et al., 1997; Cooney, Koniz-Booher, and Coly, 1997).

An interagency initiative, begun in the early 1990s, was directed toward improving the quality of service delivery and helping programs to serve their clients better. The Maximizing Access and Quality (MAQ) effort was spearheaded by USAID and involved its cooperating agencies in population (Shelton, Davis, and Mathis, 1998). The initiative helped to identify unnecessary medical barriers to family planning that limit the quality of and access to services. Medical barriers were defined as practices that use a medical rationale but result in an impediment to or denial of contraceptive use that cannot be scientifically justified. Examples of medical barriers include inappropriate age and parity criteria for determining eligibility to use certain contraceptive methods. As a result of the work under the MAQ initiative, more than 30 countries have revised and disseminated new service delivery guidelines. WHO has also reviewed its criteria for use of contraceptive methods and issued medical eligibility criteria for contraceptive methods that reflect the importance of quality of care in programs (WHO, 1996).[21] The MAQ effort and the work of WHO have contributed to research and "projects addressing every aspect of quality including management, service delivery, training, and technical guidance" (Kols and Sherman, 1998).

The research and program efforts on quality of care presented here, while only a sampling of recent work, underscore the challenges that programs face in assessing quality of care; being sensitive to clients' health, needs, and rights; and ensuring adequate quality of care. In addition, a recent article has shed light on a related but neglected as-

---

[21]The methods covered in the WHO guidelines include pills, injections, Norplant implants, female sterilization, vasectomy, IUDs, condoms, spermicides, diaphragms and cervical caps, natural family planning or fertility-awareness methods, and LAM.

pect of quality of care: the role of the provider perspective on the delivery of family planning and reproductive health services (Shelton, 2001). While programs are giving considerable attention to client perspectives, Shelton calls for more research on who providers are, how they view their roles in the delivery health services, what constraints they face in performing their roles, and how to engage providers as agents of change for improving the quality of programs. Efforts to measure and to improve quality of care are ongoing issues for all service delivery programs in countries around the world and for the international donor community as well (Miller et al., 1997). A further research challenge is studying the relationship between efforts to improve quality of and access to services and the use of contraception to help couples meet their reproductive goals. A few studies have endeavored to assess the effects of improved quality, and initial results appear promising.

REPRODUCTIVE HEALTH

Concerns about women's health and welfare and about human rights in the face of national demographic goals in some countries (discussed in Chapter Three and preceding sections of this chapter) contributed to a major shift in the framework for population policy and programs and the context in which family planning programs were considered. The pivotal event marking this change was the 1994 UN ICPD held in Cairo.

This new framework for population policy and programs, developed and championed by women's health advocates and feminists, shifted the emphasis previously given to the burden of population growth and high fertility on overall development to the welfare and rights of individuals. In giving prominence to individual rights, it gave particular attention to women's right to reproductive autonomy and empowerment to enable women to secure this right. The ICPD and the resulting Program of Action downplayed the implications of rapid population growth as a key factor for economic development and the existing consensus among governments. However, the Program of Action did consider the important links between population, economic growth, and sustainable development, including impacts on the environment. The unprecedented level of NGO participation at ICPD, especially of women's health and rights advocates from both developed and developing countries, helps to explain the extent to which women's issues were considered at the conference and emphasized in the Program of Action (McIntosh and Finkle, 1995).

In the ICPD's Program of Action, representatives of 180 countries agreed to the goal of universal access to reproductive health information and services by 2015. The Program of Action endorsed the broader context of reproductive health instead of the narrow approach of family planning. Family planning was considered one of the basic reproductive health services, along with maternal health care (safe pregnancy, safe abortion where legal, and women's nutrition), prevention of STDs, and adolescent reproductive health. A vision of reproductive health that is embodied in the ICPD's Program of Action is that "every sex act should be free of coercion and infection, every pregnancy should be intended, every birth should be healthy" (Tsui, Wasserheit, and Haaga, 1997, p. 1). The ICPD Program of Action and subsequent UNFPA reports make it clear that reproductive health is viewed as a reproductive right[22] and a basic human right (United Nations, 1995; UNFPA, 1997, 1999a). Further, it recognized that achieving reproductive health and reproductive rights are closely related to the attainment of other social rights and opportunities, such as the education of girls and gainful employment.

Following the 1994 UN Conference, the international donor community generally embraced the broader context of reproductive health in its population assistance programs. For some donors, including the UNFPA and the World Bank, the articulation of the "population problem" also changed. In a new mission statement adopted by UNFPA in 1996, references to population problems, which had been part of UNFPA's mandate since 1973, were avoided entirely. However, the statement says, "UNFPA is convinced that meeting these

---

[22]Refer to footnote 2 on p. 11 of this report for UNFPA's definition of reproductive rights. An increasing number of states has begun to address reproductive rights in national laws, in constitutions, and in their institutional procedures. For example, national constitutions in Colombia and South Africa explicitly guarantee certain reproductive rights. A number of governments are revising their population and development strategies to emphasize individual needs and rights (UNFPA, 1997).

goals—safeguarding and promoting reproductive rights, gender equity and male responsibility, empowerment of women, promoting the well-being of children . . . —will contribute to improving the quality of life and to the universally accepted aim of stabilizing world population" (United Nations, 1996, p. 595). Thus, while the official UN position backs away from addressing population growth directly, it acknowledges the desirability of not only lower growth but no growth in world population.

After three decades of funding for population programs that were largely concerned with slowing population growth to enhance economic development, the World Bank altered its strategy in response to the new approaches called for by the ICPD in Cairo. The change links population to poverty reduction and social development. Which population factors are important (the need to slow population growth or to cope with the implications of rapid fertility decline, an aging population, and/or urban growth) depends on the setting. The new strategy also places support for family planning within the broader context of reproductive health. It responds to a more client-centered, rights-based approach and moves away from support of countries' demographic targets and controls in the implementation of family planning programs (World Bank, 2000). Family planning is still viewed as a "merit good" by the World Bank in that governments should provide such services to ensure equity, i.e., so the poor have access to these and other health services that they otherwise might not have (Merrick, 2000a).

IPPF took the broader context of reproductive health and the new framework for reproductive rights developed at the ICPD and prepared its own Charter on Sexual and Reproductive Rights. The Charter was endorsed by the IPPF Members' Assembly in 1995. The charter lays out 12 fundamental principles that are intended to promote and protect these rights. The first is the "Right to Life," in that "no woman's life should be put at risk or endangered by reason of pregnancy." Others include "The Right to Privacy," which includes the right to make autonomous decisions regarding one's sexual and reproductive life; "The Right to Decide Whether or When to Have Children;" and "The Right to Health Care and Health Protection" including clients' rights to "information, access, choice, safety, privacy, confidentiality, dignity, comfort, continuity, and opinion" (IPPF, 1996). The Charter was printed in English, French, Spanish, and

Arabic and has been used by members in many countries represented by those languages. In addition, IPPF members in 20 countries have translated the charter into other languages in their efforts to increase attention to reproductive rights (Newman, 2000a).[23]

USAID joined the general move toward more client-centered approaches to family planning and also the shift to the broader context of reproductive health for its family planning assistance. A fourth objective was added to the Agency's Population and Health Strategy; namely, "to make programs responsive and accountable to the end-user" (i.e., the client) (Maguire, 1994). Three of five strategic objectives of USAID's Center for Population, Health, and Nutrition are part of reproductive health: "increased use by women and men of voluntary practices that contribute to reduced fertility; increased use of key maternal health and nutrition interventions; and increased use of improved, effective, and sustainable responses to reduce HIV transmission and to mitigate the impact of the HIV/AIDS pandemic" (USAID, 2000). The prevention and treatment of STDs is part of the Center's work in reproductive health.

Several research efforts have been carried out in response to the endorsement of reproductive health in the Program of Action at the 1994 ICPD. The NAS conducted a review of the magnitude of reproductive health problems facing developing countries and of interventions designed to address those problems (Tsui, Wasserheit, and Haaga, 1997). The four principle reproductive health problems were (1) significant levels of unwanted or mistimed births (20 to 40 percent of births), (2) an estimated 20 million unsafe abortions, (3) almost 600,000 pregnancy-related maternal deaths (abortion is the leading cause of maternal death), and (4) rising rates of STD and HIV infection.[24] The main service areas of reproductive health programs that address these problems are pregnancy and contraceptive ser-

---

[23]The following member countries have translated the charter: Bulgaria, Cambodia, China, Czech Republic, Estonia, Greece, Hungary, India, Indonesia, Italy, Japan, Lithuania, Malaysia, Netherlands/Belgium (collaborated on a Dutch version), Poland, Portugal, Republic of Korea, Russia, Thailand, and Turkey.

[24]There are other areas of international concern with important health implications such as sexual violence, sexual exploitation of children, and female genital mutilation. The NAS report provides information on the extent of these problems.

vices, delivery care for mothers and children, and prevention and management of STDs. None of these service areas is new, and many national health programs already provide these services. The ICPD's emphasis on reproductive health calls for greater attention to this array of services according to a given country's problems. In general, what is implied is a reorganization or new grouping of services that takes advantage of synergies among programs, and in some settings, new services are needed. The NAS report concludes that additional organizational and financial resources are essential for the reproductive health initiative to succeed, and that further experimentation, research, and evaluation are required to determine what organization or combination of services is most effective.

A research-related effort developed indicators on reproductive health for use in evaluating programs (Bertrand and Tsui, 1995). While reproductive health encompasses many different types of services and country programs emphasize different service areas, indicators were developed for the following: safe pregnancy, STD/HIV prevention, women's nutrition, breast-feeding, and adolescent reproductive health services.[25] Operations research has also been carried out to improve reproductive health services in many countries (Shane, 1998). For example, studies of postabortion care were carried out in Bolivia, Honduras, Mexico, and Peru from 1995 to 1998 to assess the current state of postabortion care services and to introduce and evaluate different interventions designed to improve the quality and effectiveness of services (Population Council, 1998b).

A number of research efforts have involved case studies of different countries to assess how reproductive health programs were being implemented.[26] In one such assessment, local researchers carried out case studies in Brazil, India, Morocco, and Uganda (Ashford and Makinson, 1999). Even though only a few years had passed since the ICPD, all four case studies reported progress in terms of increased

---

[25]The selection of reproductive health topics responded to program areas of USAID's Center for Population, Health, and Nutrition, and the process of developing indicators was carried out by the USAID-supported EVALUATION Project. An earlier effort led to the publication of a handbook of indicators for family planning (Bertrand, Magnani, and Knowles, 1994).

[26]For other assessments, see Hardee et al. (1999), WEDO (1999), HERA (1998), UNFPA (1999a), and Forman and Ghosh (2000).

political commitment to reproductive health and in terms of changes in service delivery. Needless to say, the degree of progress varied among countries. The challenges ahead, not the least of which is the cost and sustainability of the expanded reproductive health focus, are considerable, if not daunting, in some settings.

Among the general conclusions of this assessment were that the ICPD Program of Action, or the "Cairo agenda," reaffirmed efforts already under way to provide family planning as part of a broader approach to health care, and that it served as a catalyst for change in some countries (removal of targets in India and clarification of the legal status of abortion services in Brazil[27]). It was observed that there has been a general change in the environment in which reproductive health goals are pursued because there is more involvement of NGOs and an increasing role of women's organizations. Among the changes noted in health services were the increased efforts to improve the quality of service delivery and to integrate family planning and other reproductive health services. For example, in Uganda, 40–50 percent of providers in rural health centers have been trained in reproductive health, including prevention and treatment of STDs. The authors of the Uganda case study noted that this comprehensive training had "greatly improved providers' skills, confidence, and attitudes toward clients seeking services. There is evidence that these changes have led to greater use of reproductive health services as well as increased client satisfaction" (Mirembe, Ssengooba, and Lubanga, 1998, p. 26). In Morocco, improvements in specific areas of reproductive health were noted for use of prenatal care and family planning services, and in the percentage of births attended by trained assistants. But at the same time, it was observed that great inequalities in access to reproductive health care existed between urban and rural areas of Morocco (Belouali and Guédira, 1998).

An additional observation from the case studies was that the reform of the health sector (which includes decentralization of health services in Brazil and Uganda) has been an enabling factor to imple-

---

[27]The Brazilian penal code of 1940 authorized abortions in cases of rape and life-threatening circumstances to the mother. Despite the law, women's access to abortion in actual practice was limited to only one of these two cases (those involving life-threatening circumstances to the mother). Efforts to clarify the difference between the abortion law and actual practice began in 1991 (Corrêa, Piola, and Arihlha, 1998).

menting a more comprehensive reproductive health approach in Brazil, but has added to the complexity of making hoped-for changes in Uganda, where the lack of skilled manpower and inadequate health infrastructure are severe constraints. Some of the progress in reproductive health has been possible with increased donor funding. This has been so in India with World Bank funding for the Reproductive and Child Health project and in Uganda where donor financing supports most of the general health and reproductive health programs.[28]

The implications of the reproductive health approach for family planning programs are several. First, placing family planning within the context of reproductive health should mean that programs are more responsive to the range of reproductive health needs with a concomitant reduction in emphasis on contraceptive services and less attention to demographic goals for family planning. While more resources are called for to support the reproductive health agenda and were forthcoming in the first several years after ICPD, donor support has not continued to rise to meet the challenges set forth in 1994 (Forman and Ghosh, 2000). Unless funding prospects improve, existing resources will be spread more broadly, and this, in all likelihood, will dilute the potential impact of the reproductive health initiatives, including family planning programs.

---

[28]The major reproductive health programs funded by donors in Uganda included safe motherhood; family planning; STD/HIV prevention; adolescent health; information, education, and communication (IEC) activities; infrastructure development; and training of providers. Multilateral donors included the World Bank, UNFPA, UNICEF, and WHO, and bilateral donors included the United States, Great Britain, and Denmark (Mirembe, Ssengooba, and Lubanga, 1998, p. 22).

Chapter Five

OTHER HUMAN RIGHTS CONCERNS

This chapter reviews two issues in the development of family planning programs that are related to human rights. The preceding discussions of the demographic rationale and the broader context of reproductive health for family planning noted the significance of human rights considerations. The controversies, criticisms, and research presented in this chapter deal with other issues related to human rights—those based on fears of cultural intrusion stemming from the activities of the international population movement and religious concerns and influences that are an important component of culture in many settings.

CULTURAL INTRUSION

The issue of cultural intrusion has appeared from time to time in different contexts over the past several decades. One of the first public expressions of this concern was at the 1974 UN population conference. Many of the government representatives from developing countries attending the conference reacted to what was seen as an attempt by a few developed countries to impose their definition of the international population agenda. In addition, charges of cultural intrusion, based on perceptions of Western aid supporting family planning programs as a way to contain the numbers of people living in developing countries, came from leftists in Latin American countries in the 1970s and from militant Muslims. Some of the concerns also presumed that couples in many developing countries were not interested in regulating their fertility (e.g., for cultural reasons such as a preference for sons) and that many couples were averse to using contraception. Through the mid-1980s, many African government officials were wary of promoting family planning programs because they didn't want to promote "institutions regarded as foreign or as incompatible with African culture" (Caldwell, Orubuloye, and Caldwell, 1992, p. 215). As more agencies—including bilateral donors such as USAID, and international organizations such as UNFPA and the World Bank—entered the field and provided population assistance, there was concern among those who did not share the growing consensus about the need to address the population problem.

Some feminists attacked the approach of the international population movement in assisting in the development of population policies and programs in developing countries. These critics held that such policies and programs were externally driven, developed in a "top-down, technocratic approach" that relied on "experts" rather than on consultation with the groups that would be most affected (Dixon-Mueller, 1993, p. 83). They called for an approach that was women-centered, that was based on the conditions of women's lives, on quality reproductive health services, and that would involve listening to what women said about their needs and the constraints on meeting those needs. Further, these critics stated that women's rights and health activists needed to be part of the process of developing and monitoring policies and programs.

The validity of the concern about cultural intrusion is not simple to determine since it does not depend on scientific evidence. Rather, its validity rests on the extent to which underlying goals and strategies for public policy are held in common by recipient and donor nations and on the nature of the process of policy formulation in any given country. As more and more developing countries adopted policies favoring lower population growth and lower fertility, supported family planning programs, and accepted international population assistance, it was safe to assume that there were such common understandings. At the same time, critics have charged that donor assistance was of sufficient magnitude that it influenced policymakers in developing countries to be more interested in addressing the population problem than they would have been otherwise (Warwick, 1982; Hartman, 1987; Demeny, 1988). Other analysts of the role of population policies in developing countries counter this criticism by presenting case studies of policy formulation suggesting that the process is complex and that donor influence is overrated by critics (Jain, 1998).

Regardless of the validity of the claim of cultural intrusion, the evolution of family planning programs suggests there has been an increasing awareness of these concerns. There have been three types of responses to these concerns by the international population movement that are discussed in this chapter. First, the extensive survey programs produced information on the demand for family planning (i.e., that many couples wanted to use and would use contraception) that verified the desire for regulating fertility in many countries (see Chapter Two and Table 2.4). Second, much research has been carried out to study the influence of culture and to design culturally sensitive family planning and health programs. These efforts show that care has been taken to ensure the design of appropriate interventions in a number of settings. Evidence from this research, including pilot and experimental programs, is presented next. Third, the design and implementation of intervention programs has increasingly emphasized the need for local participation, including the participation of women.

CULTURAL SENSITIVITY IN FAMILY PLANNING PROGRAMS

Interest in cultural factors related to family planning programs reflected perceptions of cultural intrusion into the affairs of developing countries, criticism of a technocratic approach that gave too little attention to the conditions of women's lives and listening to women's needs, and religious concerns about contraception. Another aspect of the interest in culture was whether family planning programs were sensitive to cultural and social influences in their design and implementation in different settings. Detractors of family planning programs have criticized those responsible for developing policies and programs for either minimizing the importance of culture or seeing it as an obstacle to be overcome (Warwick, 1982). Renewed interest in the cultural sensitivity of programs surfaced during the 1990s in concert with the concerns about the quality of programs and attention to clients' needs and rights.

Understanding the role of culture in fertility change has been a long-standing issue for population scientists. Frank Lorimer, nearly 50 years ago, saw the importance of studying cultural conditions well in advance of the establishment of family planning programs in developing countries (with the exception of the program established in India in 1952): "Any public policy directed toward lowering fertility, to be effective, must not only provide efficient and acceptable means of controlling fertility, but must also be concerned with the development of 'background conditions' favorable to such control" (Lorimer, 1954, p. 251). John Caldwell's wealth flows theory again brought social and cultural factors to the demographic analysis of fertility change (Caldwell, 1982).[1] The fertility decline experienced in many countries has been determined by economic factors, but its timing and pace have major social and ideological components. Further, organized family planning programs were seen as part of the social system contributing to changes in fertility (Caldwell and Caldwell, 1997).

Ronald Freedman also wrote of the profound effect that culture, the system of beliefs that guide behavior in each society, has on all aspects of fertility (Freedman, 1987b). Further, a distinction was made between the social and cultural factors that influenced reproductive behavior (the desire to control the number of offspring and the spacing of births) and other factors that influenced family planning programs such as political support (Freedman and Berelson, 1976). Understanding the specific elements of the culture and social setting that affect reproduction and family planning programs was deemed essential for the appropriate design and implementation of such programs (Freedman, 1987b).[2]

---

[1]The wealth flows theory distinguishes two types of societies that are defined by the direction of the wealth flows: (1) societies based on family production in which wealth flows from younger to older generations, children contribute to familial production, and high fertility is beneficial; and (2) societies based on labor market production in which wealth flows to the younger generation, children become dependents and an economic burden to the family, and lower fertility is desirable. In this theory, Westernization plays a major role in the onset of the transition to fertility decline. Westernization is partly characterized by European concepts of family relationships (the importance of the nuclear as opposed to the extended family) and mass schooling, which is another cause of erosion of traditional family relationships.

[2]Social setting has been recognized as having an important effect on the infrastructure of family planning programs. It was believed that many countries did not have the ability to develop a strong program because the administrative capacity and the political will were not sufficient (see Chapter Two, Table 2.3).

Chapter Two of this report described the variation in the strength of family planning programs in developing countries, and noted that this variation reflected the influence of social, cultural, and institutional factors on programs. A microanalysis of socioeconomic and cultural constraints to the effective organization and delivery of family planning services in rural Bangladesh found that many of the factors that resulted in a low demand for family planning services (e.g., the status of women and the level of female education) also constrained the effective delivery of services (Koenig and Simmons, 1992).

Another dimension of culture that bears on program implementation is that there are cultural differences in how societies view the role of governments. Generally, governments in Western countries are reluctant to interfere with parental decisions about family size, certainly in terms of limiting size (exceptions being pro-natalist policies and incentives adopted in France and Romania), but this has not necessarily been the case in Eastern countries (such as China, Indonesia, and Singapore) and more paternalistic societies such as Mexico.[3]

In examining reproduction and family planning programs, the issue of cultural relevance or sensitivity is complex. This is partly because there are many sociocultural influences in a given country or setting. These influences include ethnicity, religion, whether people live in urban or rural areas, gender, age, and martial status and customs. The meaning of cultural sensitivity may depend on *whose* culture or *which* cultures are being considered. In addition, sociocultural

---

[3]Caldwell sees "social orderliness" as a key characteristic of Asian culture and a factor in the dramatic fertility transition in the "Asian arc" of countries from India through Southeast Asia to China and South Korea (Caldwell, 1993). Furthermore in the Asian arc countries, the "ruling elites have long claimed the right to provide moral leadership and now do so in the reproductive field" (Caldwell and Caldwell, 1997, p. 293). McNicoll describes two features of state influence in Asian countries: *regularity* (orderliness of state authority) and *duress* (the use of political or administrative pressure or even physical coercion) (McNicoll, 1997). He groups states by those having a high degree of orderliness (China, Taiwan, South Korea, North Korea, Thailand, and Indonesia) and those with a high level of duress (China, Indonesia, and India [during the Emergency period of 1975–1977]) (McNicoll, 1997). Both China and Indonesia were characterized by both orderliness and duress and experienced dramatic fertility change; other Asian countries with a high degree of orderliness also experienced rapid fertility decline.

influences change over time, especially in societies that are changing and developing. Developing countries are increasingly exposed to new ideas and messages through modern communication such as soap operas. These "permeate cultural barriers to varying degrees almost everywhere and can have destabilizing consequences for traditional cultures" (Freedman, 1987b, p. 58).

The status of women and men's role in decisionmaking may be important factors, along with women's autonomy and empowerment, that affect a range of reproductive behaviors including the adoption of contraception (Dixon-Mueller, 1998). Gender roles and power relationships between males and females are additional aspects of the social and cultural context in which programs are designed and implemented (UNFPA, 2000b).

In some cases, the cultural factors may involve contradictory influences as in the case of youth needs and parents' willingness to deal with them. For example, in settings where a sizable percentage of unmarried young women are sexually active and at risk of pregnancy and STDs (as in Ghana, Tanzania, and Jamaica, where one-quarter or more are [Singh et al., 2000]), the needs of these youth for reproductive health services may not be addressed if their families or communities oppose or do not recognize this behavior. The problem of addressing the needs of youth is especially critical in southern African countries where there are increasing levels of HIV infection.[4]

Given the various cultural influences, some groups in a given setting will be more ready to adopt modern practices; others will be less so or resistant. Family planning programs have been based on the presence of a vanguard of individuals who were poised to adopt modern contraception. For example, as early as 1968–69, attitudes about family size among women in Colombia revealed that 65 percent of women preferred smaller families than they were having (Estrada et al., 1972).[5] It was these women who were poised to limit their family

---

[4]Various factors—such as sexual coercion, the negative image of condoms, gender imbalance in sexual decisionmaking, and peer pressure concerning sexual performance—make the challenge of addressing youth needs in these countries all the more difficult (Varga, 1999).

[5]In 1969, the total fertility rate in Colombia was 6.0 children per woman, while the ideal number of children (the "most convenient number of children") that women re-

size and to take advantage of a program of modern contraception. Which women have represented those in the vanguard varies across countries. In some countries (e.g., Sri Lanka and Taiwan), it was older, higher-parity women[6] who wanted to limit childbearing and who were the first to adopt contraception; in another population (i.e., the island of Bali in Indonesia), it was younger, lower-parity women who were first to adopt contraception (Freedman and Berelson, 1976).

There are numerous social and cultural reasons that may explain why some individuals are more wary of or resistant to adopting contraception, and such factors may play a role in people's ability to seek and use family planning services. "In some settings, for example, potential clients may be fearful of utilizing nearby services because of negative social stigma attached with doing so, may be wary of certain procedures (e.g., pelvic examinations), or may be unable to seek services because women are not permitted to travel alone to obtain contraceptive services or supplies" (Bertrand, Magnani, and Knowles, 1994, p. 104). In a number of developing country settings, women resort to clandestine use of birth control because they fear the opposition of their husbands and other relatives (Castle et al., 1999).

Many research studies have been conducted over the years to assess cultural barriers to the use of contraception and to understand the nature of unmet needs. Several more recent efforts are discussed here. Barriers to contraceptive use among indigenous groups in Latin America included factors such as distrust of outsiders, particular belief systems that foster fatalism about childbearing, religious opposition to contraception, and low status of women and the dominant role of men in decisionmaking about family planning (Terborgh et al., 1995). A study in Nepal looked at the reasons why women's fertility preferences and their contraceptive behavior often appear contradictory. In-depth interviews with 98 rural Nepalese women and their husbands revealed that what on the surface appears to be

---

ported in survey data was 3.4 for urban women and 4.4 for rural women (Estrada et al., 1972).

[6]Parity refers to the number of children previously born alive to a woman; for example, women who are referred to as women of parity five are those who have had five children up until now.

contradictory behavior may actually reflect quite rational decisions based on women's assessment of their risk of becoming pregnant and the risks of using different methods of family planning. For example, sterilization has been an important part of family planning in Nepal (46 percent of users of modern methods have been sterilized as of 1996), and some respondents equated use of contraception with sterilization and thus decided not to use contraception since they were not prepared to terminate their childbearing (Stash, 1999).

It is important to note that not all social and cultural factors serve to inhibit changes in contraceptive use and fertility. The following two examples from Thailand and Zimbabwe describe family planning programs that benefited from environments that were conducive to contraceptive use and fertility change.

Thailand. The Thai national family planning program is viewed as having played an important role in "precipitating and facilitating reproductive change" (Knodel, Chamratrithirong, and Debavalya, 1987). In addition to the family planning program's role, these authors note a number of cultural factors that were conducive to fertility change. In Thailand, individual couples, not the parents or kin, were largely responsible for the choice of a spouse, the timing of marriage, and the start of childbearing as well as the number of children. Thus the locus of decisionmaking in matters of marriage and childbearing was with the couple. The status of women in Thailand was also favorable to fertility decline in that literacy was essentially universal, and female labor-force participation rates were high. Further, husbands and wives had a relatively equal relationship within the family. Increasing education aspirations of parents for their children also encouraged smaller family size. Finally, the predominant religion (Thai Buddhism) was not pro-natalist nor did it have prohibitions on the use of birth control.[7] The contraceptive prevalence rate in Thailand increased from 44 percent in 1980 to 69 percent in 1996, and fertility declined from 6.3 children per woman

---

[7]A Buddhist principle separates religious and worldly matters so that contraception is outside of the religious sphere in Thailand. Islam is the religion of a small percentage of Thais and thus had only a minor influence on national contraceptive and fertility rates. In general, Muslims have had higher fertility than Buddhists in Thailand (Knodel, Chamratrithirong, and Debavalya, 1987).

in 1964–1965 to 4.9 in 1974–1976 (Knodel et al., 1987) and to an estimated 1.9 in 2000 (Population Reference Bureau, 2000).

Zimbabwe. The National Family Planning Program of Zimbabwe has played an important role in the increase in contraceptive use, which rose from 38 to 54 percent between 1984 and 1999. The adoption of modern contraception in Zimbabwe, principally the pill, was promoted for reasons of birth spacing and thus has been considered as a "modern" replacement for—and compatible with—strong traditional norms that favored birth spacing through long periods of postpartum sexual abstinence. Fertility levels have also dropped because of a number of factors including Zimbabwe's relatively high level of development, a high level of education for women, and relatively low levels of infant and childhood mortality. These factors along with the availability of contraception have contributed to a rapid fertility decline from a TFR of 5.5 children per woman in 1988–1989 to 4.3 in 1994 and further to 4.0 in 1999—a decline of 1.5 children in 11 years (Kirk and Pillet, 1998; ORC Macro, 2001).

PILOT PROJECTS TO DEVELOP CULTURALLY APPROPRIATE DELIVERY SYSTEMS

The history of family planning programs includes a number of noteworthy examples of pilot projects that tested different approaches to the delivery of family planning services and helped to ensure that they were culturally appropriate. These pilot projects sought to understand the social and cultural setting in order to find the most appropriate way to appeal to couples and to structure programs.

Taiwan. The classic pilot study in Taiwan in the 1960s "tested the waters" by surveying a small group of women about their fertility desires and their interest in methods to avoid additional births and by offering contraception. Initial concerns were expressed by a leading Taiwanese sociologist-demographer about the feasibility of gathering information on women's fertility and by an important public health official about the acceptability of establishing a public family planning program. These early concerns proved to be unfounded. The benchmark KAP survey confirmed that women were willing to answer questions about their fertility preferences and were interested in methods of avoiding additional births. The pilot family planning services project had no adverse political problems and led to the large-scale Taichung study, which "tested out many different approaches and examined the relevance of different cultural assumptions" (Freedman, 1987b, p. 60). For example, the study tested the effectiveness of different approaches to couples about family planning services and different modes of communication about the services. Among the results, it was "found that approaching both wife and husband did not significantly increase the acceptance or the continuation use rate, as compared with approaching the wife alone" (Freedman, 1987b, p. 60). The Taichung study was conducted prior to the establishment of the national family planning program. Thus, as the national program developed, it was based on an accurate assessment of the cultural conditions and constraints.

There are several more recent examples of pilot projects that were designed based on an understanding of cultural influences.

Matlab, Bangladesh. Associated with the field research station of the International Centre for Diarrhoeal Disease Research, Bangladesh (ICDDR,B), the Maternal Child Health and Family Planning (MCH-FP) Project in the rural subdistrict of Matlab has come to be known for its unusual achievements in increasing use of contraception and inducing fertility decline in a traditional, agrarian, and economically disadvantaged area in Bangladesh. The MCH-FP Project represents a classic example of the importance of an experimental project with treatment and control areas that tested different approaches. Since 1977, the MCH-FP Project in the treatment area has provided more accessible and higher-quality family planning services than the standard government services provided in the comparison (control) area. Whereas married women in the comparison area were supposed to receive the standard visits every two months from female welfare assistants who provide counseling and supply pills and condoms, in the treatment, or MCH-FP, area, community health workers visited married women of reproductive age every two weeks to provide counseling about family planning services and deliver injectables, pills, and condoms at the doorstep.

An earlier project in the Matlab area was not successful because it tested "ill-informed and sociologically inappropriate strategies" in a traditional setting where demand was weak (Phillips et al., 1988, p. 328).[8] However, the MCH-FP Project took a very different approach in the design of the experiment, which led to sustained changes in contraceptive use and fertility.

The key to the MCH-FP Project's success was designing strategies for making contraceptives available that took into account an understanding of the factors inhibiting women's use. Among these is the system of purdah that limits women's mobility outside the family compound and thus limited access to clinic-based services. Even though the previous project has provided distribution of contraceptives to households, the role of female workers as change agents was new in the MCH-FP Project. They provided not only contraceptives but also support to clients through regular household visits. The household visits were the basis of the workers' establishing rapport with their women clients: The clients discussed the realities of their daily lives, and the workers provided support for using contraception by allaying fears about methods of contraception (e.g., their side effects) (Phillips et al., 1988). The success of the design also involved providing ample support to the female village workers who in the early years of the program encountered opposition to their activities because they challenged the traditional practices limiting women's

---

[8]The earlier Contraceptive Distribution Project (CDP) tested the effect of making contraceptives (principally pills and condoms) available. It was a test of "the supply-side hypothesis in its most bare-bones manifestation—a pills-to-all-doorsteps inundation of the population...it represented a deliberate attempt to *minimize* the role of the supply side [i.e., the supply-side constraints]: little strategic planning was attempted, orientation and training of workers was minimal, and the organization of work routines, staff management, and work systems development were oriented toward commodity distribution, rather than toward client services" (Phillips et al., 1988, p. 323). A later analysis provided an alternative interpretation about why the earlier CDP was viewed as a failure (Caldwell and Caldwell, 1992). The Caldwells' analysis was based on the fact that the CDP had provided a limited number of methods. Their explanation for the CDP's failure highlighted the role of user demand for more contraceptive methods (especially injectables, subsequently found to be very popular among women in this region), and they questioned primary emphasis to supply and management factors given by Phillips and others.

involvement in activities beyond the family and movement outside their hamlet (Simmons, Mita, and Koenig, 1992).[9]

Changes in contraceptive prevalence and fertility have been substantial in the MCH-FP Project area. Before 1978, contraceptive use was less than 10 percent and the total fertility rate was more than 6.5 births per woman. By 1996, prevalence was 68 percent, and fertility had declined to fewer than 3.0 births per woman. In addition, the incidence of abortion declined in the MCH-FP area in recent years and was 31 percent lower than in the comparison area in 1995. Since contraceptive prevalence was much higher in the treatment area than the comparison area (68 percent compared with 47 percent), the differences in the levels of abortion "may be related to the differences in the intensity and quality of maternal and child health and family planning services in the two areas" (Ahmed, Rahman, and van Ginneken, 1998, p. 130). A recent analysis showed a lower incidence of abortion in the treatment or project area is due to the lower incidence of unintended pregnancy, which is the result of higher levels of contraceptive use and lower levels of unmet contraceptive need (Rahman, DaVanzo, and Razzaque, 2001).

While recognizing the positive impact that use of contraception has had on women's lives in Bangladesh, one recent critique has noted that the "home delivery system has reinforced the patriarchal status quo" (where women are isolated, economically dependent, and have low status relative to men) (Schuler et al., 1996, p. 76). Schuler et al. recommended a gradual shift in the strategy of the family planning program that would place more emphasis on clinic facilities to help draw women out of their homes and also to allow them to get a broader range of information and services than they receive in their homes. This strategy assumed that empowerment would increase through a clinic-based approach and that by increasing empower-

---

[9]Over time, the community accepted the employment of women as field-workers in the MCH-FP Project (Simmons, Mita, and Koenig, 1992). Based on the success of the MCH-FP Project in Matlab, a Maternal Child Health and Family Planning Extension Project was launched in 1982 that replicated the Matlab service approaches in two districts under the auspices of the Bangladesh Ministry of Health and Social Welfare. Female outreach workers were a component of the Extension Project, and an analysis of the 1984–1993 period showed that the intensive outreach helped to introduce contraceptive services and also to sustain contraceptive use over time (Phillips, Hossain, and Arneds-Kuenning, 1996).

ment, use of contraception would also increase. The national program has moved in the last few years to be more clinic-based and woman-centered, with an emphasis on reproductive and child health (Crane, 2000).

Phillips and Hossain (1998, p. 21) have urged caution, however, with the policy recommendation to emphasize clinic facilities given that "no experimental study has demonstrated gender benefits over the current program" of household visits. In contrast, their analysis showed that women's status was enhanced by the household outreach services.

A recent study of the change to clinic-based delivery of services showed that contraceptive levels were being maintained and even increasing (Routh et al., 2001). The authors pointed out that women left their homes to obtain contraceptives at clinics, contrary to the norms of purdah, suggesting that women were no longer dependent on home-based delivery of contraceptives.

Three pilot projects in Ghana, Peru, and Guatemala, discussed below, have also addressed the need to create a supportive environment and have done so through deliberate, but very different, strategies of community participation. "Participatory" approaches have been accorded increasing attention in recent years in family planning and reproductive health programs.[10] What defines this approach is the participation of local communities, intended recipients of services, and key stakeholders (policymakers, key administrators, religious leaders, and so forth) in project design and implementation.

Navrongo, Ghana. The Navrongo Community Health and Family Planning (CHFP) Project, begun in 1994, is being implemented in a rural district in Northern Ghana where the social, cultural, and economic institutions favor childbearing early in marriage and high fertility. The pilot project works within the Ministry of Health, which is seeking guidance from the field research about how to improve health service delivery and how to involve the community in this

---

[10]The WHO strategy for contraceptive introduction, which was discussed in Chapter Four (pp. 96–97), is another example of the incorporation of participatory approaches that address cultural sensitivity (Spicehandler and Simmons, 1994).

effort. The CHFP Project attempts to develop and test culturally appropriate systems of family planning service delivery and generate demand for and improve the provision of health services in a traditional community (Nazzar et al., 1995; Binka, Nazzar, and Phillips, 1995). The project has an experimental design with five distinct geographical areas that enable testing and comparing different combinations of services (community-based primary care and family-planning services, typical Ministry of Health services with upgraded clinical facilities and staff training, and one district that serves as a control) (DaVanzo, Lule, and Satia, 1997).

Among the initial steps taken before designing the pilot project were in-depth interviews and focus groups with community members: women under age 30, older women, young men, heads of compounds and their wives, and opinion leaders. These interviews were used partly to explore "if the highly developed traditional structure of a rural African community could be an organizational resource for establishing effective community health services" (Nazzar et al., 1995, p. 308). The initial research showed that the community wanted health services, and thus family planning services were delivered under this umbrella. Subsequently, village chiefs became part of the pilot project study team—"advising the project on strategy, organizing community action, and participating in program deliberations. They, in turn, convene meetings with project staff, divisional chiefs, and lineage heads on matters requiring the attention of the community" (Nazzar et al., 1995, p. 313). These meetings (called durbars) have been helpful in legitimizing project activities and engaging the community in the project's implementation.

The CHFP had two phases of implementation. The micro pilot, or Phase I, conducted in 1996 in three villages with an intensive outreach through community health officers, found that contraceptive prevalence increased from a minimal level to 10 percent. Those adopting contraception appeared to be substituting modern methods for traditional means of fertility regulation such as postpartum abstinence and prolonged breastfeeding. The project's attention to village participation in the community-based services also appeared to increase interest and support for the services (Phillips et al., 1997). Preliminary data from the scaled-up Phase II intervention also showed an increase in the use of contraception to 10 percent and almost universal immunization of children in villages where the community workers were active. Furthermore, the process of participatory planning and implementation successfully generated community support for the project (DaVanzo, Lule, and Satia, 1997).

One critique of the CHFP Project's approach to community participation is that it accommodates the traditional patriarchal structure in which men monopolize the social institutions (Schuler, 1999). By working within the existing community structure, the project manages (rather than alters) gender constraints to reproductive health. However, recent evidence from Navrongo shows that women are increasingly involved in the community participation by attending the durbars and serving as members of the political action committees that help advise the project (Schuler, 1999).

As is appropriate for a project working within the public health care system, the primary goal of the CHFP Project has been to provide health services that include family planning. Although changing gender relations and increasing women's empowerment were not key project objectives, such changes have occurred. Recent evidence from the Navrongo project shows that the use of contraception has generated tensions in gender relations in some families (with husbands as well as the extended family) because women have greater autonomy over their reproduction (Bawah et al., 1999). Thus the project has served to alter gender relations, and in some cases the project's staff has provided additional support to women to protect them from men's anger about their contraceptive use (Bawah et al., 1999). While the project staff was not surprised by men's reactions, given the deeply held expectations about women's reproductive behavior, the staff felt a responsibility to help women and reach out to men to address gender tensions.

The approach to community participation in the Navrongo project appears justified based on a study of why some women adopted contraception. In this setting, the individual preferences of women and men to limit or space childbearing were not important given the strong traditions of marriage and family building. Since individual autonomy is clearly subordinate to the collective will of the family and community, the project's approach of community participation has helped to foster social legitimacy for family planning (Phillips et al., 1997). The project's approach raises an interesting research and ethical issue for social policy. Should intervention programs respect and work within an existing social structure, or should they try to change it?

ReproSalud, Peru. The ReproSalud project, begun in 1996, is implemented by an NGO of Peruvian feminists, Movimiento Manuela Ramos. The project works with community-based women's groups in economically disadvantaged rural and peri-urban areas in Peru. Its approach to community participation contrasts with the Navrongo project because it was designed explicitly to address women's empowerment and rights, through community-based programs. As in Navrongo, reproductive health services were underutilized in the selected project areas. The project's design assumes that there are underlying constraints to the use of reproductive health services that include gender inequalities and lack of empowerment for women. It assumes that a community-based approach will improve the quality of services because women will demand better services (as a result of the project's interventions) and that it will enhance the use of contraceptive and other reproductive health services (Crane, 2000).

Through the project, support is given to community-based groups in three areas: reproductive health, income generation, and advocacy. The process of developing and carrying out subprojects is intended to be an empowering experience for the women involved. Local groups do their own "needs identification" and then select a reproductive health problem to address. They then develop a subproject. In the project's first two years, all subprojects were educational, consisting of training promoters on reproductive health topics, who in turn train others in the community and women's organizations in nearby communities. At the request of some women's groups, men have also been included in some of the training, which includes reproductive health and women's rights, so men have become more aware of gender issues. In sum, the project enables women at the grassroots or community level to decide what their needs and issues are, how to address them, and whether men should be involved in the reproductive health project (Schuler, 1999).

A 1999 qualitative field assessment of the project's work in 13 communities showed very promising results in terms of (1) women's improved knowledge of reproductive and contraceptive methods, and also (2) changing social norms in communities with low contraceptive prevalence in that it was increasingly appropriate to discuss these subjects. Furthermore, the project's emphasis on women's rights and new gender roles within communities helped to improve spousal communication about family planning. There was also evidence of increased intention to use contraception and evidence of increased use. Finally, the project's emphasis on clients' rights has improved client-provider interaction. Ministry of Health providers reported that the "women's increased abilities as clients" had made their jobs easier and more fulfilling (USAID/Peru, 1999).

Quiché Birth Spacing Project, Guatemala. This pilot project represents an interesting example of one designed to reach indigenous groups, an important hard-to-reach population, and one that was based on an assessment of clients' attitudes and needs. The Mayan populations in Guatemala are ethnic groups whose use of health services and especially family planning is low because of the language barrier, since most health centers are staffed only by Spanish-speaking personnel (Terborgh et al., 1995). In an effort to increase access to services for these Mayan groups, the Asociación Pro-Bienestar de la Familia (APROFAM), a private family planning association, designed a comprehensive intervention.

The project supported several intervention strategies that were identified following focus groups with Mayan men and women. Through the focus group discussions, project staff gained a better understanding of the cultural values placed on fertility, attitudes toward birth spacing and contraceptive use, as well as impressions of APROFAM. Among the key strategies for implementing the pilot project were the participation of bilingual volunteer promoters who resided in the local communities where they were working and also the doubling of the number of promoters. Other intervention strategies included improved quality of services through training, supervisory visits, and continuous supply of contraceptives; increasing awareness of the benefits of birth spacing through information, education, and communication (IEC) activities (including radio broadcasts and a video in the Maya-Quiché language); and improving the image of APROFAM in the community by working with other established development agencies. These project strategies represented an important influx of resources, and they had a significant effect on the knowledge and behavior of these Mayan women of reproductive age. Their awareness of at least one modern method of contraception increased dramatically from 42 to 95 percent, and use of modern contraception rose from 4 to 14 percent. Even though contraceptive use rose, it was still relatively low compared with other Latin American populations, suggesting that contraceptive demand is not strong among the Guatemalan Mayans. While this experimental project demonstrated increases in knowledge and use of contraception, the level of resources and the multiple intervention strategies required to achieve these changes will make it very difficult to meet the needs of this hard-to-reach population on a larger scale and an ongoing basis (Bertrand et al., 1999).

OTHER EXAMPLES OF ACTIVITIES THAT HAVE ENHANCED THE CULTURAL APPROPRIATENESS OF FAMILY PLANNING PROGRAMS

There are numerous other examples of specific activities that are considered to have enhanced the cultural appropriateness of family planning programs. Of course, specific activities that are well designed and include a strong participatory approach do not necessarily make an entire program one that is culturally sensitive.

IEC activities have been found to be an important component of effective programs (Robey, Piotrow, and Salter, 1994). These activities are typically based on audience research to ensure that the messages and the media used to reach audiences are appropriate. In Mexico, a special study was conducted among young adults and their parents in six indigenous ethnic groups to determine needs for IEC in reproductive health. These results were then used by the rural social security program (IMSS-Solidaridad) in developing both strategies and messages on reproductive health that would be appropriate for youth given the local preferences and customs (Cabral et al., 1998).

During the last several years in India, several states including Gujarat, Rajasthan, and Uttar Pradesh have used a more participatory strategy in their population planning activities aimed at implementing a target-free approach in state family planning programs. For example, the initiation of District Action Plans in six districts of Uttar Pradesh has involved the participation of public- and private-sector groups including local NGOs, cooperative societies, religious leaders, and village heads (pradhans), one-third of whom are female in these districts (Raghunath, 1999; Narayana et al., 1999).

Special efforts have been undertaken in a number of countries to reach adolescents, both females and males, who are considered underserved groups. Traditionally, most family planning programs have been directed toward the needs of married women. However, there is a substantial number of adolescents who are having sex before marriage, whose risk of unintended pregnancy and STDs is thus high, and yet whose access to services is limited. There are an increasing number of adolescent reproductive health projects throughout the world, and many of these have a participatory approach as an explicit part of their design and implementation (Senderowitz, 1999).

Some of these are school-based programs that focus on increasing knowledge of adolescent sexuality and prevention of pregnancy and STDs; some also deal with gender roles (including programs of the Ministries of Education in Colombia and Kenya). Many family planning affiliates of IPPF have special programs for adolescents that provide both education and services. In Colombia, for example, Profamilia has adolescent centers in a number of cities that provide information and services on reproductive health (prevention of STDs as well as pregnancy) to youth—both boys and girls—ages 13–19 (Senderowitz, 1999). A four-country program in Africa (Botswana, Cameroon, Guinea, and South Africa) tested the impact of youth-oriented social marketing to raise awareness of sexual and reproductive health problems and to encourage young people to take preventive action (Ashford, 2000).

A concern that has been raised about providing adolescents with information and services related to family planning and reproductive health is that these efforts will lead to increased sexual activity and cause promiscuity. Contrary to these fears, the evidence shows that such programs do not increase sexual activity among young adults (McCauley and Salter, 1995).

Whether sufficient attention has been given to sociocultural factors in carrying out family planning programs is an open question. There are examples of "less successful" family planning programs

(Pakistan, Bangladesh in the 1970s, and India[11]) which "too early became standardized, rather inflexible programs applied uniformly on a national basis, often regardless of local readiness, local conditions, availability of qualified personnel, or the need to learn and to adjust to local and distinctive national conditions" (Freedman, 1987b, p. 63). Lessons learned from the conduct of pilot projects in Bangladesh helped turn that country's family planning program into a successful effort. More recently, changes in India's Family Welfare Program, such as a more participatory approach to program planning, hold the promise of more culturally sensitive implementation strategies.

There are numerous family planning pilot projects and programs, several of which have been reviewed here, that have given considerable attention to social and cultural influences and to variations in different settings. Some of these examples have illustrated the complexity of dealing with cultural factors in the course of promoting new ideas and behaviors. Despite efforts to be culturally sensitive, pilot programs that have encouraged change in the status quo have, at the same time, caused tensions that were simply unavoidable. Experience, such as that from Bangladesh, has shown that, over time, the tensions have diminished as innovative behaviors were accepted, adopted more broadly, and became the norm.

RELIGIOUS CONCERNS AND INFLUENCES

Religion is an important part of culture in many societies, and religious traditions have played a role in the articulation of population policies and in the development of family planning programs. Religious doctrine and beliefs have influenced individual attitudes and behavior on family size and use of contraception and thus to some extent have affected individuals' and couples' reproductive rights. The Catholic and Muslim religious traditions are highlighted in this discussion.

---

[11]It should be noted that some states in India, such as Tamil Nadu and Karnataka, have been considered to have more effective programs that those in other states (Koenig and Khan, 1999).

While Roman Catholic perspectives on population policy and contraception have played a role in Catholic teaching historically, it was not until the 20th century that they became more prominent. The views of the Catholic Church on population policy were aired at the UN's World Population Conference in 1974 and at subsequent UN population conferences in 1984 and 1994.[12] Though the concern about the relationship between population and resources was acknowledged, the church's position was that it was "morally wrong and practically ineffective to isolate population as a single factor" of social and economic change (Reich, 1995). The church clearly favored the view that development was essential to improve the well-being of the masses and for reasons of social justice. But, the Catholic Church, being pro-natalist, was opposed to government and international donor interference in such a personal dimension of family life as would be represented by family planning. Contraception has been seen as immoral since it would likely to lead to undesirable consequences including marital infidelity and the debasing of women (Burch and Shea, 1971). The church's opposition to artificial methods of contraception was well established in its teachings. Contraception had been condemned in 1930 in the encyclical Casti Connubii of Pope Pius XI (Noonan, 1986). The opposition to contraception (except for periodic abstinence), contraceptive sterilization, and abortion for whatever reason was reaffirmed in Pope John Paul's Humanae Vitae of 1968 (Burch, 1995).

The influence of the Catholic Church's position on contraception made it more difficult for some countries in Latin America during the 1970s to adopt population policies and develop national family planning programs. While it may be assumed that official Catholic doctrine on contraception has had some influence on individual practices, how much influence is not clear. However, it seems to have had little impact in Catholic countries with very low birth rates

---

[12]The Holy See, as the political entity of the Catholic Church, holds the status of a nonmember state permanent observer at the United Nations. This status allows the Holy See to participate as a governmental representative at UN meetings. Some population assistance advocates are lobbying the United Nations to change the status of the Holy See to that of an NGO, which would prevent its participation in intergovernmental conferences in the future. At the ICPD in 1994, "the Vatican was joined by several conservative Islamic countries such as Saudi Arabia, Iran, and Sudan to register opposition to increasing access to contraception for women" (Amin, Diamond, and Steele, 1997, p. 287).

such as Italy or Spain, which at 1.2 children per woman, now have the lowest fertility rates in the world.[13]

The teachings and beliefs of other religious traditions on issues of population, family size, and contraception are complex and diverse. Classical Islam, Hinduism, and Confucianism are fairly permissive about the use of birth control, but have religious traditions that favor large families. There is considerable variation among Muslim countries in their positions on population and family planning because of the interaction between religious teaching, local cultural traditions, and national policies. For example, governments in both Indonesia and Egypt have active family planning programs supported by senior Islamic officials, while the government of Saudi Arabia limits access. Scholars of Islamic law have generally helped to legitimize population policies in most Muslim countries and have provided an Islamic rationale for most modern methods of contraception. Fatwas (formal legal opinions) have endorsed contraception, although most Islamic jurists forbid one method, sterilization, when used only for purposes of contraception. In Egypt and Indonesia, fatwas endorsing contraception have been used to support government birth-control policies and programs (Esposito, 1995, p. 1979).[14] "In Bangladesh, the family planning programme follows a strategy of co-opting religious leaders through motivation and education. This strategy appears to have been successful in defusing initial opposition to family planning" (Amin, Diamond, and Steele, 1997, p. 269).

---

[13]In the United States, fertility differences between Catholic and non-Catholics narrowed beginning in the mid-1950s, so that by 1982 the differences were very small (Goldscheider and Mosher, 1988). Subsequent research, which examined births from 1977–1987, showed that the total fertility rate for non-Hispanic white Catholic women was 1.64 children per woman compared with 1.91 for non-Hispanic white Protestant women. Generally, Hispanic women have higher fertility than non-Hispanic women (1.55 children ever born compared with 1.2), but there is essentially no difference between Catholic and Protestant Hispanic women. Differences among Protestant dominations showed that fundamentalist Protestants have 1.56 children ever born compared with 1.19 for other Protestants, but when controls for age, education, income, and marital duration are included in the analysis, the difference drops to 0.14 and is not statistically significant (Mosher, Williams, and Johnson, 1992).

[14]In Indonesia, it has been noted that "the national family planning programme's concessions to Islam (such as refusing to adopt sterilization as a national programme method . . .) is not matched by concessions to other religious traditions which lack political power" (Hull and Hull, 1997, pp. 402-403).

There are differences in Islam between official religious decrees and the more conservative responses of local religious leaders and popular beliefs. Since there is no organized hierarchy and no scholarly consensus, local religious leaders and their followers hold a variety of opinions. Some local religious leaders have condemned contraception, and Islam has served to reinforce traditional, pro-natalist beliefs and practices in areas where social conditions make large families desirable. Popular religious beliefs among Muslims may also affect reproductive behavior. For example, beliefs about "kismet," or fate, and the idea that "Allah appoints each couple the children they are to have" have led to reluctance among some Muslim couples to use family planning (Green, 1995, p. 1975). At times and in some Muslim countries, the "criticisms of local religious leaders combine with voices of militant Muslims who attack the government-sponsored family-planning program and Western aid as a conspiracy to limit the size of the Muslim community in order to contain and dominate it more effectively" (Esposito, 1995, p. 1981).

The impact of religious concerns and influences on family planning programs in developing countries over the past 35 years is varied. Papal pronouncements on contraception undoubtedly had an effect on population policies and programs in many Catholic countries and on individual behavior as well. In general, however, family planning programs—including national government programs—were established despite church teachings on contraception and, over time, have provided services to growing numbers in the Catholic countries of Latin America and in the Philippines, the only Catholic country in Asia (Keely, 1994). Among Islamic countries, there is considerable variation in the "extent to which religious leaders cooperate with government-sponsored fertility-control programs" (Esposito, 1995, p. 1981). Moderate-to-strong family planning programs exist in Bangladesh, Egypt, Iran, Indonesia, Morocco, Tunisia, and Turkey.

In other Islamic countries, including Afghanistan, Saudi Arabia, Somalia, Sudan, and Yemen, contraceptive prevalence is low. It is possible that more-conservative Islamic leaders have had a greater influence on family planning programs and reproductive behavior in these countries, but other social, cultural, economic, and political factors may also have played a role.[15]

Assessing the validity of religious concerns is generally outside the boundaries of what science can address. However, the implications of religious doctrine and beliefs for population policies and family planning programs can be understood through scientific study. Research in a number of countries has also shown that religious doctrine has changed when religious leaders have been involved in the discussion of population policies and programs because it has engendered greater understanding and support.

---

[15]In analyzing reproductive choice in Islam, Obermeyer shows the strong influence of changing political strategies on women's options in two Islamic countries, Tunisia and Iran. She concludes that Islamic doctrine was an instrument of state policy because it was used by the ruling political powers and was influenced by changes in economic, political, and social spheres to legitimate conflicting positions on gender and reproductive choice (Obermeyer, 1994, p. 49).

Chapter Six

CONCLUSIONS, LESSONS LEARNED, AND POLICY IMPLICATIONS

Thirty-five years after the beginning of the international movement for family planning in developing countries, the majority of developing countries have policies to lower population growth and reduce fertility. The vast majority of developing countries support access to family planning services through organized programs that provide contraception to women and men. This support, coupled with that from international donor and funding organizations, has been substantial and has contributed to the increased availability of family planning services. Over half of the world's couples in developing countries uses contraception, and in many countries the level of contraceptive prevalence is over 70 percent. The majority of couples from Catholic, Islamic, and Buddhist countries uses contraception. Family planning has become a norm in many societies and cultures and for many families. However, in most countries of sub-Saharan Africa, the level of contraceptive prevalence is low. In only two countries, Mauritius and South Africa, is contraceptive prevalence over 50 percent, and in only five additional countries—Botswana, Kenya, Namibia, Zambia, and Zimbabwe—is prevalence over 25 percent.

While the majority of the world's couples uses contraception, not all needs for contraception have been met by family planning programs. It is estimated that about 17 percent of women of reproductive age in developing countries have an unmet need for contraception; that is, they desire to limit or space future births, but they are not practicing contraception. Satisfying these unmet needs would help reduce fertility, an outstanding national goal in many developing countries, and it would help couples achieve their individual reproductive goals.

International support to family planning programs has been predicated on three goals—demographic, health, and human rights—since the earliest days of population assistance. The relative importance of these goals has varied over the past 35 years. Since the 1994 UN ICPD, family planning has generally been accepted within the broader context of reproductive health, and greater importance has been given to reproductive health as a human right. Developing countries now face considerable challenges as they address the ICPD goal of universal access to reproductive health by 2015.

The evolution of family planning programs, of which the broader context of reproductive health is only the most recent development, shows the dynamic history of one of the more significant social and health interventions in the second half of the 20th century. Family planning programs have been subject to a number of controversies and criticisms. The responses to the criticisms and controversies, including research, have helped programs become more effective and more responsive.

ARE THE CRITICISMS OF FAMILY PLANNING PROGRAMS VALID?

The criticisms of family planning programs relate to all three objectives or rationales for programs: demographic, health, and human rights. Were these criticisms valid? Several were, and several were not. Whether the criticisms were valid or not, considerable research was generated to address them. The question of scientific validity is not relevant for the few criticisms that were based on differing ideological perspectives. The following summarizes the criticisms and their validity.

Demographic Objectives

Population Growth and Economic Development. The relationship between population growth and economic development has been a controversial subject for decades in part because of differing political and ideological views and in part because the scientific evidence was inconclusive. But newer studies carried out in the 1990s have found that slower population growth and lower fertility can matter a great deal for economic growth in developing countries. At the same time, appropriate economic policies are crucial for realizing the "demographic bonus" that comes because of changes in a population's age structure that result when fertility rates fall. This research evidence supports assumptions made in the mid-1950s about links between population growth and development.

Effectiveness of Family Planning Programs. Part of the debate about the role of family planning programs as an effective public policy rested on whether programs could deliver on the promise of increasing contraceptive use and reducing fertility. Research spanning several decades has shown that family planning programs have been an effective public policy for facilitating widespread use of contraception and lowering fertility. The extent of change is partly due to the level of social and economic development, but there has also been a clear, independent effect of programs. Evidence from pilot and experimental programs has also shown that stronger programs have led to increased contraceptive use and lower fertility. Family planning programs have been much more effective than many skeptics had presumed possible. At the same time, the variation in the strength of programs and in the level of social and economic development suggests that a continuing, concerted effort to improve and expand services is still required in many countries, especially in sub-Saharan Africa.

Demographic Goals and Human Rights. Criticism of the demographic rationale for population policies and programs (i.e., the need to reduce fertility and population growth to improve social and economic well-being) and the emphasis on numbers and targets to which it led came largely from women's rights and health advocates. These critics charged that some family planning programs were implemented in such a way that women were impeded in exercising their rights to reproductive autonomy in decisions about childbearing and contraception. The critique was valid based on the policies and programs carried out in a limited number of countries. The critique also raised a number of complex issues in terms of basic principles underlying family planning programs (voluntarism and individual welfare and rights) and national sovereignty as well as different interests (individual versus societal) in family planning programs. The criticisms have resulted in policy and program changes in many countries and have heightened attention of the international donor and funding organizations to these issues.

Population Growth or Implosion? Because of low fertility rates in a number of more-developed countries, some recent commentators on public policy have sounded an alarm about a coming population implosion. In so doing, they have questioned whether population growth is a continuing policy concern. Current estimates and projections show that there are two compelling demographic challenges for the future. The first is the continuing growth of populations throughout much of the developing world. The second is the slow decline in population size and a resulting aging of these populations in a number of developed countries. There will be a continuing need for high-quality family planning services in the former.

Health Objectives

Contraceptive Technology. Other parts of the debate over family planning concerned the possible negative effects of contraception on women's health and the focus of new contraceptive development efforts. While the number of methods available in programs has been shown to affect contraceptive prevalence, research and program experience has indicated that not all programs have provided a wide range of contraceptives to ensure method choice. In addition, not all methods are suitable for all users, sometimes because of health considerations. Thus, this concern on the part of women's health advocates and feminists was valid, and it is also one aspect of quality of care (see below).

Despite the availability of a range of simpler, safer contraceptive methods, issues about the development of new contraceptives highlighted a difference between scientists' interests in the safety and efficacy of new methods and concerns of women's health advocates about the need for more attention to the context in which methods would be used (i.e., the conditions of women's lives including gender relations). Both groups have valid points of view that are being taken into account in contraceptive development and research.

Health Benefits of Family Planning. Research has confirmed the beneficial effects of family planning on maternal and child health. Women's use of safe and effective contraception helps reduce maternal mortality by reducing the number of births and high-risk pregnancies and helps lower infant and child mortality by reducing the number of high-risk births.

Abortion. The legal status of abortion has been a source of controversy among proponents and opponents of abortion. This controversy, based on differing ideological perspectives, has spilled over onto family planning programs in many countries. A growing body of research from different countries is showing that more available and better family planning services reduces abortion. One positive consequence of the controversy over abortion is the increased attention on the part of donors and developing countries to promoting postabortion care services. Expanded access to postabortion services, including counseling about contraception, should help to reduce future abortions.

Quality of Care. The criticism that family planning programs had not given sufficient attention to quality of care is based on survey evidence of levels of unmet need and of users discontinuing use of contraceptive methods even if they continued to have a need. Other evidence from numerous research studies has confirmed that the lack of attention to quality was a valid concern. Concerted efforts have been made in the past decade to define the dimensions of quality of care, develop indicators of quality, and conduct research to assess levels of quality and the impact of interventions to improve quality. The research has shown that quality is important for programs and for individual users of contraception.

Reproductive Health Context. Women's health advocates and feminists have criticized the emphasis on family planning in population policy and programs in many developing countries and by international donor organizations. Many of their concerns, in general, were valid since most family planning programs had a singular focus on the delivery of contraception. In fact, it was probably the intensity of this focus that produced the political will and resources required to establish and expand services in many countries. These critics formed the vanguard of those seeking to shift population policy and programs from demographic objectives to human rights. The broader context of reproductive health and its link to human rights has been widely endorsed by nations around the world and international donors, and this endorsement in effect acknowledged the need for a broader policy framework.

Other Human Rights Objectives

Cultural Intrusion and Cultural Sensitivity.   Another controversy that has been aired about family planning programs was whether these programs represented a form of cultural intrusion in the affairs of developing countries on the part of developed countries. Clearly, there were "outside" influences in the process of policy formulation in the form of donor and funding assistance, but local constituencies in the developing countries themselves probably were a more important factor in the development of population policies and programs. Research has contributed to an understanding that family planning was a needed public health service and that programs could be implemented in a culturally sensitive manner. For example, survey research in scores of countries has shown that women and couples have favorable attitudes about family planning, and there is a demand for such services. Furthermore, pilot and experimental projects in a number of countries enabled testing of different approaches to determine if they would be appropriate for a given setting, and appropriate approaches have been developed in very different countries around the world.

Religious Concerns.   Religious concerns were, and still are, an important consideration for family planning programs in some countries. These concerns, which are based on religious doctrine and faith, are outside the boundaries of what scientific research can address; thus the question of their validity is not useful. Studies have been done of the impact of religion on individual attitudes and behavior and of the role of religious influences in policy formulation. These have shown great variation in the role of religion on family planning programs in developing countries. In addition, experience in a number of countries has pointed out that involving religious leaders in the development of policies and programs has led to greater understanding and support for programs.

LESSONS LEARNED

What lessons are there from this review of controversies and criticisms that can guide future public policies and health programs? A key, but obvious, lesson is the role of research. Family planning programs in developing countries have benefited greatly from a variety of research endeavors including national surveys, pilot and experimental studies, case studies, operations research, and anthropological research. International donors, such as USAID, have funded much of this research.

National survey data have demonstrated that women and couples want to control their fertility and an increasing number have done so. Survey data have also shown that there is an outstanding (or unmet) need for contraception among an important segment of the populations. Survey data in combination with anthropological and in-depth studies helped to identify reasons why some women discontinued using contraception and also why there were unmet needs. For example, this research has produced greater understanding that while most women desire some measure of control over their fertility, they are not always able to do so. The extent to which women are able to turn their intentions into actions— to make reproductive decisions—varies according to the context of their lives.

Other research studies have helped to specify the primary components of service delivery programs and to identify strengths and weakness in these programs, including the need for increased quality of care. Additional research has examined whether improvements in aspects of quality of care made a difference to clients. Research studies have also confirmed that having a range of contraceptive methods leads to increased overall contraceptive prevalence and greater user satisfaction. Similarly, studies have shown that a range of service delivery strategies, including community-based or household distribution, is important for increased use, particularly in settings where the regular public health delivery system may be weak and where there are important social and cultural obstacles to the use of contraception.

Pilot and experimental studies have helped to identify the critical role of community participation in developing culturally sensitive family planning and reproductive health programs. Such participation helps to foster understanding and support from the community. Pilot and experimental projects are especially useful for testing different approaches to service delivery and for determining whether underlying assumptions (e.g., about how social and cultural factors may affect the acceptance of services) are valid.

POLICY IMPLICATIONS

Despite the enormous progress in meeting the demand for family planning services in the past 35 years, significant challenges remain in satisfying unmet needs. The size of the next generation of adolescents is estimated at about one billion, making it the largest generation in history. These youth will be entering their years of sexual activity and childbearing. They will be among the growing numbers of women and couples seeking services and with unmet needs. Satisfying their needs will add considerably to the challenges of service delivery in the future.

The new broader context of reproductive health also has major implications for the organization and financing of services. Research on different combinations of interventions (including adding new services such as prevention and treatment of STDs, HIV, and AIDS) will be critical for determining whether particular strategies are effective. Enhancing the organization of services and the research on their effectiveness will add significantly to the costs of reproductive health programs. In addition, given that health services in many countries are still relatively weak, it may simply not be feasible to expect much improvement or change in the extent of service delivery. Further, the HIV/AIDS crisis places additional demands on health assistance to the developing world (including the demand for condoms) and competes with other components of reproductive health. While international donor and funding organizations' support for population and reproductive health increased in the years immediately following ICPD, it is not meeting projected financial requirements. Without greater funding, the goal of universal access to reproductive health will not be met.

While the criticisms of the demographic rationale for population policies and programs have led to improvements in some programs, such changes do not occur quickly and uniformly, especially when policies and practices have been followed for many years in large government bureaucracies. It will be very important to monitor and evaluate the implementation of policy and program improvements. International donors, funding agencies, and NGOs can play a role in this effort, but this will only be possible if programs are open to such assessments. Similarly, the criticism of the lack of attention to quality of care in family planning programs has generated considerable interest and research designed to improve quality. However, these efforts need to be ongoing and coupled with good monitoring and evaluation research to ensure that enhanced quality becomes or remains an important objective of programs.

Finally, the increased participation of NGOs, including women's groups and health advocates, particularly in the 1990s, also has future policy implications. These groups have contributed greatly to the debates and dialogue on many critical issues (from contraceptive technology to quality of care in programs to women's involvement in the design and implementation of programs in developing countries). Donor and funding organizations as well as developing country governments need to reach out and incorporate these NGOs in both policymaking and program development.

Adamson, David M., Nancy Belden, Julie DaVanzo, and Sally Patterson, *How Americans View World Population Issues: A Survey of Public Opinion*, Santa Monica, Calif.: RAND, 2000.

Ahmed, M. Kapil, Mizanur Rahman, and Jeroen van Ginneken, "Induced Abortion in Matlab, Bangladesh: Trends and Determinants," *International Family Planning Perspectives*, Vol. 24, No. 3, 1998, pp. 128–132.

Ali, Mohamed, and John Cleland, "Contraceptive Discontinuation in Six Developing Countries: A Cause-Specific Analysis," *International Family Planning Perspectives*, Vol. 21, No. 3, 1995, pp. 92–97.

Amin, Sajeda, Ian Diamond, and Fiona Steele, "Contraception and Religiosity in Bangladesh," in Jones, Gavin W., et al., *The Continuing Demographic Transition*, Oxford: Clarendon Press, 1997, pp. 268–289.

Arid, John, "Population Studies and Population Policy in China," *Population and Development Review*, Vol. 8, No. 2, 1982, pp. 267–297.

Ashford, Lori, *Social Marketing for Adolescent Sexual Health*, Population Services International and Population Reference Bureau, 2000.

Ashford, Lori, and Carolyn Makinson, *Reproductive Health in Policy and Practice: Case Studies from Brazil, India, Morocco, and Uganda*, Washington, D.C.: Population Reference Bureau, 1999.

Askew, Ian, Barbara Mensch, and Alfred Adewuyi, "Indicators for Measuring Quality of Family Planning Services in Nigeria," *Studies in Family Planning*, Vol. 25, No. 5, 1994, pp. 268–283.

Association for Voluntary Surgical Contraception (AVSC), "Counseling, Informed Choice, Informed Consent, and the Rights of the Client," http://www.engenderhealth.org/wh/fp/iwhast. html (as of November 2001), 2000.

Barnett, Barbara, and Jane Stein, *Women's Voices, Women's Lives: The Impact of Family Planning*, A Synthesis of Findings from the Women's Studies Project, Family Health International, 1998.

Bawah, Ayaga Agula, Patricia Akweongo, Ruth Simmons, and James F. Phillips, "The Impact of Family Planning on Gender Relations in Northern Ghana," *Studies in Family Planning*, Vol. 30, No. 1, 1999, pp. 54–66.

Beamish, Julia, Yolanda Palma, and Judith R. Seltzer, *USAID Population Assistance Program in Mexico: Last Phase, 1992–1999*, Washington, D.C.: Population Reference Bureau, 2001.

Belouali, Radouane, and Najib Guédira, *Reproductive Health in Policy and Practice: Morocco*, Washington, D.C.: Population Reference Bureau, 1998.

Berelson, Bernard, "KAP Studies on Fertility," in Berelson, Bernard et al., *Family Planning and Population Programs: A Review of World Development*, Chicago, Ill.: The University of Chicago Press, 1966, pp. 655–668.

———, ed., *Family Planning and Population Programs: A Review of World Development*, Chicago, Ill.: The University of Chicago Press, 1966.

———, "Beyond Family Planning," *Studies in Family Planning*, No. 38, 1969a.

———, ed., *Family-Planning Programs: An International Survey*, New York: Basic Books, 1969b.

———, "The World Population Plan of Action: Where Now?" *Population and Development Review*, Vol. 1, No. 1, 1975, pp. 115–146.

Berer, Marge, "The Quinacrine Controversy One Year On," *Reproductive Health Matters*, No. 4, 1994.

———, "The Quinacrine Controversy Continues," *Reproductive Health Matters*, No. 6, 1995.

Bernstein, Stan, personal electronic mail communication, New York: UNFPA, August 2, 2001.

Berry, Vicky, "IPPF Members," electronic mail communication, London: IPPF, August 1, 2000.

Bertrand, Jane T., Robert J. Magnani, and James C. Knowles, *Handbook of Indicators for Family Planning Program Evaluation*, The EVALUATION Project, 1994.

Bertrand, Jane T., Karen Hardee, Robert J. Magnani, and Marcia A. Angle, "Access, Quality of Care and Medical Barriers in Family Planning Programs," *International Family Planning Perspectives*, Vol. 21, No. 2, 1995, pp. 64–75.

Bertrand, Jane, and Amy Tsui, *Indicators for Reproductive Health Program Evaluation: Introduction*, The EVALUATION Project, 1995.

Bertrand, Jane T., Sandra Guerra de Salazar, Lidia Mazariegos, Ventura Salanic, Janet Rice, and Christine Kolars Sow, "Promoting Birthspacing Among the Maya-Quiché of Guatemala," *International Family Planning Perspectives*, Vol. 25, No. 4, 1999, pp. 160–167.

Binka, Fred N., Alex Nazzar, and James F. Phillips, "The Navrongo Community Health and Family Planning Project," *Studies in Family Planning*, Vol. 26, No. 3, 1995, pp. 121–139.

Birdsall, Nancy, Allen C. Kelley, and Steven W. Sinding, eds., *Population in the Developing World Matters: Demography, Economic Growth, and Poverty*, Oxford: Oxford University Press, 2001.

Bloom, David E., David Canning, and Jaypee Sevilla, *Economic Growth and the Demographic Transition*, Santa Monica, Calif.: RAND, forthcoming.

Bongaarts, John, "The KAP-gap and the Unmet Need for Contraception," *Population and Development Review*, Vol. 17, No. 2, 1991, pp. 293–313.

———, "Do Reproductive Intentions Matter?" *International Family Planning Perspectives*, Vol. 18, No. 3, 1992, pp. 102–108.

———, "The Impact of Population Policies: Comments," *Population and Development Review*, Vol. 20, No. 3, 1994, pp. 616–620.

———, "The Role of Family Planning Programs in Contemporary Fertility Transitions," in Jones, Gavin W., John C. Caldwell, Robert M. Douglas, and Rennie M. D'Souza, eds., *The Continuing Demographic Transition*, Oxford: Clarendon Press, 1997, pp.422–444.

Bongaarts, John, W. Parker Mauldin, and James F. Phillips, "The Demographic Impact of Family Planning Programs," *Studies in Family Planning*, Vol. 21, No. 6, 1990, pp. 299–310.

Bongaarts, John, and Judith Bruce, "The Causes of Unmet Need for Contraception and Social Content of Services," *Studies in Family Planning*, Vol. 26, No. 2, 1995, pp. 57–75.

Bruce, Judith, "Fundamental Elements of the Quality of Care: A Simple Framework, *Studies in Family Planning*, Vol. 21, No. 2, 1990, pp. 61–91.

Buckner, Bates C., Amy O. Tsui, Albert I. Hermalin, and Catherine McKaig, eds., *A Guide to Methods of Family Planning Program Evaluation, 1965–1990*, The EVALUATION Project, 1995.

Bulatao, Rodolfo A., *The Value of Family Planning in Developing Countries*, Santa Monica, Calif.: RAND, 1998.

Burch, Thomas K., Book review of Robert McClory's *Turning Point: The Inside Story of the Papal Birth Control Commission, and How Humanae Vitae Changed the Life of Patty Browley and the Future of the Church*, in *Population and Development Review*, Vol. 21, No. 4, 1995, pp. 882–885.

Burch, Thomas, and Gail A. Shea, "Catholic Parish Priests and Birth Control: A Comparative Study of Opinion in Colombia, the United

States, and the Netherlands," *Studies in Family Planning*, Vol. 2, No. 6, 1971, pp. 121–136.

Cabral, Javier, A. Flores, F. Huerta, C. Baltaza, F. García, C. Orozco, and Carlos Brambila, "Encuesta de Necesidades de Información, Educación y Comunicación (IEC) sobre Salud Reproductive en Seis Etnias en México," INOPAL III, *Documentos de Trabajo*, No. 6, 1998.

Caldwell, John C., *Theory of Fertility Decline*, London: Academic Press, 1982.

———, "The Asian Fertility Revolution: Its Implications for Transition Theories," in Leete, Richard, and Iqbal Alam, eds., *The Revolution in Asian Fertility Transition*, Oxford: Clarendon Press, 1993, pp. 299–316.

Caldwell, John C., and Pat Caldwell, "The Cultural Context of High Fertility in sub-Saharan Africa," *Population and Development Review*, Vol. 13, No. 3, 1987, pp. 409–437.

———, "What Does the Matlab Fertility Experience Really Show?" *Studies in Family Planning*, Vol. 23, No. 5, 1992, pp. 292–310.

Caldwell, John C., I. O. Orubuloye, and Pat Caldwell, "Fertility Decline in Africa: A New Type of Transition?" *Population and Development Review*, Vol. 18, No. 2, 1992, pp. 211–242.

Caldwell, John C., and Pat Caldwell, "What Do We Now Know About Fertility Transition?" in Jones, Gavin W., et al., *The Continuing Demographic Transition*, Oxford: Clarendon Press, 1997.

Caldwell, John C., Barkat-E-Khuda, Bruce Caldwell, Indrani Pieris, and Pat Caldwell, "The Bangladesh Fertility Decline: An Interpretation," *Population and Development Review*, Vol. 25, No. 1, 1999, pp. 67–84.

Casterline, John B., and Steven W. Sinding, "Unmet Need for Family Planning in Developing Countries and Implications for Population Policy," Population Council, *Working Papers*, No. 135, 2000.

Castle, Sarah, Mamadou Kani Konaté, Priscilla R. Ulin, and Sarah Martin, "A Qualitative Study of Clandestine Contraceptive Use in

Urban Mali," *Studies in Family Planning*, Vol. 30, No. 3, 1999, pp. 231–248.

Center for Reproductive Law and Policy and Grupo de Información en Reproducción Elegida, "Women's Reproductive Rights in Mexico: A Shadow Report." Prepared for the Eighteenth Session of the Committee on the Elimination of All Forms of Discrimination Against Women, 1997.

Chamie, Joseph, "Trends, Variations, and Contradictions in National Policies to Influence Fertility," in Finkle, Jason L., and C. Allison McIntosh, eds., *The New Politics of Population: Conflict and Consensus in Family Planning*, Vol. 20 (Suppl.), *Population and Development Review*, 1994.

Chesler, Ellen, "Margaret Sanger and the Birth Control Movement," in Cimbala, Paul A., and Randall M. Miller, eds., *Against the Tide: Women Reformers in American Society*, Westport, Conn.: Praeger Press, 1997.

Cleland, John, Chris Scott, and David Whitelegge, *The World Fertility Survey: An Assessment*, New York: Oxford University Press, 1987.

Cleland, John, and Warren Robinson, "The Use of Payments and Benefits to Influence Reproductive Behavior," in Phillips, James F., and John A. Ross, *Family Planning Programmes and Fertility*, Oxford: Clarendon Press, 1992.

Coale, Ansley J., and Edgar M. Hoover, *Population Growth and Economic Development in Low Income Countries*, Princeton, N.J.: Princeton University Press, 1958.

Cohen, Sylvie I., and Michèle Burger, *Partnering: A New Approach to Sexual and Reproductive Health*, Technical Paper No. 3, New York: UNFPA, 2000.

Conly, Shanti, *Taking the Lead: The United Nations and Population Assistance*, Population Action International, 1996.

Conly, Shanti, and Shyami de Silva, *Paying Their Fair Share? Donor Countries and International Population Assistance*, Population Action International, 1998.

Consejo Nacional de Población (CONAPO), Poder Ejecutivo Federal, *Programa Nacional de Población 1995–2000.* Mexico City: CONAPO, 1996.

Cooney, Kristin A., Peggy Koniz-Booher, and Shirley Coly, *Taking the First Steps: The Lactational Amenorrhea Method, A Decade of Experience,* Final Report of the Breastfeeding and MCH Division of the Institute for Reproductive Health, Washington, D.C.: Georgetown University, 1997.

Corrêa, Sonia, Sérgio Piola, and Margareth Arilha, *Reproductive Health in Policy and Practice: Brazil,* Washington, D.C.: Population Reference Bureau, 1998.

Cottingham, Jane, F.C.C. Bergin, and A. Martin Hilber, "Women's Perspectives and Gender Issues," *Human Reproduction Programme Annual Technical Report 1999,* Geneva: World Health Organization, 1999.

Crane, Barbara, personal electronic mail communication, Washington, D.C.: USAID, September 2, 2000.

Curtis, Siân, and Ann K. Blanc, *Determinants of Contraceptive Failure, Switching, and Discontinuation: An Analysis of DHS Contraceptive Histories,* Macro International, Inc., Demographic and Health Surveys Analytical Reports No. 6, 1997.

Davis, Kingsley, "Population Policy: Will Current Programs Succeed?" *Science,* Vol. 158, 1967, pp. 730–739.

DaVanzo, Julie, and John Haaga, "Women in Development: Issues for the Latin American and Caribbean Region," Latin America and the Caribbean Technical Department, World Bank, 1991.

DaVanzo, Julie, Elizabeth Lule, and Jay Satia, "Review of the Community Health and Family Planning Project of the Navrongo Health Research Centre," Program Review for the Rockefeller Foundation, 1997.

Demeny, Paul, "On the End of the Population Explosion," *Population and Development Review,* Vol. 5, No. 1, 1979, pp. 141–162.

————, "Social Science and Population Policy," *Population and Development Review*, Vol. 14, No. 3, 1988, pp. 451–479.

————, "Policies Seeking a Reduction of High Fertility: A Case for the Demand Side," *Population and Development Review*, Vol. 18, No. 2, 1992, pp. 321–332.

Department of Family Welfare, Government of Andhra Pradesh, *Andrah Pradesh State Population Policy: A Statement and a Strategy*, 1997.

Department of Family Welfare, Government of Rajasthan, *Population Policy of Rajasthan*, 1999.

Diaz, Margarita, Ruth Simmons, Juan Diaz, Carlos Gonzales, Maria Yolanda Makuch, and Debora Bossemerer, "Expanding Contraceptive Choice: Findings from Brazil," *Studies in Family Planning*, Vol. 30, No. 1, 1999, pp. 1–16.

Dixon-Mueller, Ruth, *Population Policy and Women's Rights: Transforming Reproductive Choice*, Westport, Conn.: Praeger Press, 1993.

————, "Female Empowerment and Demographic Processes: Moving Beyond Cairo," *Policy and Research Papers*, No. 13, International Union for the Scientific Study of Population, 1998.

DKT International, "1999 Contraceptive Social Marketing Statistics," Washington, D.C.: 2000.

Donaldson, Peter, J., *Nature Against Us: The United States and the World Population Crisis, 1965–1980,* Chapel Hill, N.C.: The University of North Carolina Press, 1990.

Douglas, Emily Taft, *Margaret Sanger: Pioneer of the Future*, New York: Holt, Rinehard and Winston, 1970.

Drennan, Megan, "Reproductive Health: New Perspective on Men's Participation," *Population Reports*, Series J, No. 46, Baltimore, Md.: Johns Hopkins School of Public Health, Population Information Program, 1998.

Dwivedi, Hermant, and Daya Kishan Mangal, "The Implementation of the Reproductive and Child Health Programme in Rajasthan: A Review of Experience," The POLICY Project, New Delhi: The Futures Group International, draft paper, 2000.

Eberstadt, Nicholas, "The Population Implosion," *Foreign Policy Magazine*, March/April 2001.

Ehrlich, Paul R., *The Population Bomb*, New York: Ballantine Books, 1968.

El Gebaly, Hassan, Ron Hess, Carol Brancich, and Cynthia Waszak, "Egypt's Gold Star Program: Improving Care and Raising Expectations," in Kols, Adrienne J., and Jill E. Sherman, "Family Planning Programs: Improving Quality," *Population Reports*, Series J, No. 47, Baltimore, Md.: Johns Hopkins University School of Public Health, Population Information Program, 1998, pp. 20–21.

Esposito, John L., "Religious Traditions: Islamic Perspectives," in Reich, Warren Thomas, editor-in-chief, *Encyclopedia of Bioethics*, revised edition, New York: Simon & Schuster Macmillan, 1995, pp. 1977–1981.

Estrada, Alcides et al., "Resultados Generales; Encuesta Nacional de Fecundidad," Bogota, Asociación Colombia de Facultades de Medicina, Division de Medicina Social y Población, 1972.

Fathonah, Siti, *Patterns of Contraceptive Use in Indonesia*, National Family Planning Coordinating Board, Jakarta, Indonesia and Macro International Inc., Calverton, Md., 2000.

Finger, William, and Sarah Keller, "Norplant: The Need for Training and Counseling," *Network*, Family Health International, Vol. 16, No. 1, 1995.

Finkle, Jason L., and Barbara B. Crane, "The Politics of Bucharest: Population, Development, and the New International Economic Order," *Population and Development Review*, Vol. 1, No. 1, 1975, pp. 87–114.

————, "Ideology and Politics at Mexico City: The United States at the 1984 International Conference on Population," *Population and Development Review*, Vol. 11, No. 1, 1985, pp. 1–28.

Ford Foundation, "Yunnan Province's Women's Reproductive Health and Development Program," Beijing, no date.

Forman, Shepard, and Romita Ghosh, eds., *Promoting Reproductive Health: Investing in Health for Development,* Boulder, Colo.: Lynne Reinner Publishers, 2000.

Freedman, Ronald, "The Social and Political Environment, Fertility, and Family Planning Program Effectiveness," in Lapham, Robert, and George Simmons, eds., *Organizing for Effective Family Planning Programs*, Committee on Population, Washington, D.C.: National Academy Press, 1987a.

————, "The Contribution of Social Science Research to Population Policy and Family Planning Program Effectiveness," *Studies in Family Planning*, Vol. 18, No. 2, 1987b, pp. 57–82.

Freedman, Ronald, and Bernard Berelson, "The Record of Family Planning Programs," *Studies in Family Planning*, Vol. 7, No. 1, 1976, pp. 1–40.

Freedman, Ronald, and Deborah Freedman, "The Role of Family Planning Programmes as a Fertility Determinant," in Phillips, James F., and John A. Ross, *Family Planning Programmes and Fertility*, Oxford: Clarendon Press, 1992.

Gardner, Robert, Richard D. Blackburn, Ushma D. Upadhyay, "Closing the Condom Gap," *Population Reports*, Series H, No. 9, Baltimore, Md.: Johns Hopkins School of Public Health, Population Information Program, 1999.

Germain, Adrienne, and Jane Ordway, *Population Control and Women's Health: Balancing the Scales,* New York: International Women's Health Coalition in cooperation with the Overseas Development Council, 1989.

Gillespie, Duff, "International Population: The Continuing Challenge," Paper presented at the 29th Air Force Academy Assembly in 1987 cited in Wallace, Helen M., and Giri Kanti, *Health Care of Women and Children in Developing Countries*, Oakland, Calif.: Third Party Publishing Company, 1990.

Goldberg, Howard I., Malcolm McNeil, and Alison Spitz, "Contraceptive Use and Fertility Decline in Chogoria, Kenya," *Studies in Family Planning*, Vol. 20, No. 1, 1989, pp. 17–25.

Goldscheider, Calvin, and William D. Mosher, "Religious Affiliation and Contraceptive Usage: Changing American Patterns, 1955–1982," *Studies in Family Planning*, Vol. 19, No. 1, 1988, pp. 48–57.

Goliber, Thomas J., "Population and Reproductive Health in Sub-Saharan Africa, *Population Bulletin*, Vol. 52, No. 4, 1997.

Grant, James P., "UNICEF and the Health of Mothers and Children," in Wallace, Helen M., and Giri Kanti, *Health Care of Women and Children in Developing Countries*, Oakland, Calif.: Third Party Publishing Company, 1990.

Green, Ronald M., "Religious Traditions: Introduction," in Reich, Warren Thomas, editor-in-chief, *Encyclopedia of Bioethics*, revised edition, New York: Simon & Schuster Macmillan, 1995, pp. 1974–1976.

Gu, Baochang, "Reorienting China's Family Planning Program: An Experiment on Quality of Care Since 1995," paper presented at the annual meeting of PAA, March 2000.

Hardee-Cleaveland, Karen, and Judith Banister, "Fertility Policy and Implementation in China, 1986–88, *Population and Development Review*, Vol. 14, No. 2, 1988, pp. 245–286.

Hardee, Karen, Maureen Clyde, Olivia P. McDonald, Wilma Bailey, and Michele T. Villinski, "Assessing Family Planning Service-Delivery Practices: The Case of Private Physicians in Jamaica," *Studies in Family Planning*, Vol. 26, No. 6, 1995, pp. 338–349.

Hardee, Karen, Kolila Agarwal, Nancy Luke, Ellen Wilson, Margaret Pendzich, Marguerite Farrell, and Harry Cross, "Reproductive Health Policies and Programs in Eight Countries: Progress Since Cairo," *International Family Planning Perspectives*, Vol. 25 (Suppl.), 1999, pp. 52–59.

Harkavy, Oscar, *Curbing Population Growth: An Insider's Perspective on the Population Movement*, New York: Plenum Press, 1995.

Hartman, Betsy, *Reproductive Rights and Wrongs: The Global Politics of Population Control and Contraceptive Choice*, New York: Harper and Row Publishers, Inc., 1987.

Hatcher, Robert A., Ward Rinehart, Richard Blackburn, and Judith S. Geller, *The Essential of Contraceptive Technology*, Baltimore, Md.: Johns Hopkins School of Public Health, Population Information Program, 1997.

Health, Empowerment, Rights, and Accountability (HERA), *Confounding the Critics: Cairo, Five Years On*, HERA Conference Report, 1998.

Helzner, Judith F., "Men's Involvement in Family Planning," *Reproductive Health Matters*, No. 7, 1996, pp. 146–154.

Henshaw, Stanley K., "Abortion Incidence and Services in the United States, 1995–1996," *International Family Planning Perspectives*, Vol. 30, No. 6, 1998, pp. 263–270.

Hermalin, Albert I., "Spatial Analysis of Family Planning Program Effects in Taiwan, 1966–72," Papers of the East–West Population Institute, No. 48, 1978.

———, "The Context of Family Planning Evaluation: An Evolutionary Perspective," paper prepared for a seminar in Costa Rica for a forthcoming IUSSP volume on *Methods for Evaluating Family Planning Programs*, 1997.

Hermalin, Albert I., and Barbara Entwisle, eds., *The Role of Surveys in the Analysis of Family Planning Programs* (Proceedings of an IUSSP seminar held in Bogota, Colombia, October 1980), Liege, Belgium: Ordina Editions, 1982.

Hermalin, Albert I., and Zeinab Khadr, "The Impact of Family Planning Programs on Fertility: A Selective Assessment of the Evidence," paper prepared for the Conference on Assessing the Past for the Future: Family Planning Policy, Programs, and Resources, Bellagio, Italy, 1996.

Hernandez, Daniel J., *Success or Failure? Family Planning Programs in the Third World*, Westport, Conn.: Greenwood Press, 1984.

Hieu, Do Trong et al., *An Assessment of the Need for Contraceptive Introduction in Vietnam*, WHO/HRP/ITT, Geneva: World Health Organization, 1995.

Hight-Laukaran, Virginia, Miriam H. Labbok, Anne E. Peterson, Veronica Fletcher, Helena von Hertzen, and Paul F. A. Van Look, "Multicenter Study of the Lactational Amenorrhea Method (LAM): II. Acceptability, Utility, and Policy Implications," *Contraception*, Vol. 55, 1997, pp. 337–346.

Hodgson, Dennis, "Demography as Social Science and Policy Science," *Population and Development Review*, Vol. 9, No. 1, 1983, pp. 1–34.

Hoesni, R. Hasan M., "The National Family Planning Coordinating Board (BKKBN) of Indonesia, Central Level Policy Review," The POLICY Project, 2000.

Hull, Terence H., and Valerie J. Hull, "Politics, Culture, and Fertility: Transitions in Indonesia," in Jones, Gavin W., et al., *The Continuing Demographic Transition*, Oxford: Clarendon Press, 1997.

Hull, Terence H., and Meiwita B. Iskandar, "Indonesia," in Shepard, Forman, and Romita Ghosh, eds., *Promoting Reproductive Health: Investing in Health for Development*, Boulder, Colo.: Lynne Reinner Publishers, 2000, pp. 79–109.

Hunter, Lori, *The Environmental Implications of Population Dynamics*, Santa Monica, Calif.: RAND, 2000.

Huntington, Dale, and Sidney Ruth Schuler, "The Simulated Client Method: Evaluating Client–Provider Interactions in Family Planning Clinics," *Studies in Family Planning*, Vol. 24, No. 3, 1993, pp. 187–193.

Huntington, Dale, Ezzeldin Osman Hassan, Nabil Attallah, Nahid Toubia, Mohamed Naguib, and Laila Nawar, "Improving the Medical Care and Counseling of Postabortion Patients in Egypt," *Studies in Family Planning*, Vol. 26, No. 6, 1995, pp. 350–362.

Indian Institute of Health Management Research, Ford Foundation, Population Council, and University of Michigan, "Indo-China

Dialogue on Managing the Transition to Quality of Care," Report of a meeting, September 1999.

Interim Working Group on Reproductive Health Commodity Security, *Meeting the Challenge: Securing Contraceptive Supplies,* Washington, D.C.: Population Action International, 2001.

International Planned Parenthood Federation (IPPF), *IPPF Charter on Sexual and Reproductive Rights,* London, 1996.

———, *The Review: IPPF Annual Report 1998,* London, 1999.

International Planned Parenthood Federation/Western Hemisphere Region (IPPF/WHR) and AVSC International, "Five Case Studies for the Symposium on Male Participation in Sexual and Reproductive Health: New Paradigms," Oaxaca, Mexico, 1998.

International Women's Health Coalition, "Beyond Cairo and Beijing: Rights," http://www.iwhc.org/b_rights.html (as of February 2000), 2000.

Issacs, Stephen L., "Incentives, Population Policy, and Reproductive Rights: Ethical Issues," *Studies in Family Planning,* Vol. 26, No. 6, 1995, pp. 363–367.

Jain, Anrudh, "Fertility Reduction and the Quality of Family Planning Services," *Studies in Family Planning,* Vol. 20, No. 1, 1989, pp. 1–16.

———, ed., *Do Population Policies Matter? Fertility and Politics in Egypt, India, Kenya, and Mexico,* New York: The Population Council, 1998.

Jain, Anrudh, Judith Bruce, and Sushil Kumar, "Quality of Services, Programme Efforts and Fertility Reduction," in Phillips, James F., and John A. Ross, *Family Planning Programmes and Fertility,* Oxford: Clarendon Press, 1992.

Jain, Anrudh, Judith Bruce, and Barbara Mensch, "Setting Standards of Quality in Family Planning Programs," *Studies in Family Planning,* Vol. 23, No. 6, 1992, pp. 392–395.

Jones, Gavin W., R. M. Douglas, John C. Caldwell, and R. M. D'Souza, *The Continuing Demographic Transition*, Oxford: Clarendon Press, 1997.

Keely, Charles B., "Limits to Papal Power: Vatican Inaction After Humanae Vitae," in Finkle, Jason L., and C. Alison McIntosh, *The New Politics of Population: Conflict and Consensus in Family Planning*, Vol. 20 (Suppl.), *Population and Development Review*, 1994.

Kim, Young Mi, Fitri Putjuk, Endang Basuki, and Adrienne Kols, "Self-Assessment and Peer Review: Improving Indonesian Service Providers' Communication with Clients," *International Family Planning Perspectives*, Vol. 26, No. 1, 2000, pp. 4–12.

Kirk, Dudley, and Bernard Pillet, "Fertility Levels, Trends, and Differentials in Sub-Saharan Africa in the 1980s and 1990s," *Studies in Family Planning*, Vol. 29, No. 1, 1998, pp. 1–22.

Knodel, John, Aphichat Chamratrithirong, and Nibhon Debavalya, *Thailand's Reproductive Revolution: Rapid Fertility Decline in a Third-World Setting*, Madison, Wisc.: University of Wisconsin Press, 1987.

Knodel, John, Napaporn Havanon, and Werasit Sittitrai, "Family Size and the Education of Children in the Context of Rapid Fertility Decline," *Population and Development Review*, Vol. 16, No. 1, 1990, pp. 31–62.

Koenig, Michael A., and Ruth Simmons, "Constraints on Supply and Demand for Family Planning: Evidence from Rural Bangladesh," in Phillips, James F., and John A. Ross, *Family Planning Programmes and Fertility*, Oxford: Clarendon Press, 1992.

Koenig, Michael A., Mian Bazle Hossain, and Maxine Whittaker, "The Influence of Quality of Care upon Contraceptive Use in Rural Bangladesh," *Studies in Family Planning*, Vol. 28, No. 4, 1997, pp. 278–289.

Koenig, Michael A., and M. E. Khan, *Improving Quality of Care in India's Family Welfare Programme: The Challenge Ahead*, New York: The Population Council, 1999.

Koenig, Michael A., Gillian H. C. Foo, and Ketan Joshi, "Quality of Care Within the Indian Family Welfare Programme: A Review of Recent Evidence," *Studies in Family Planning*, Vol. 31, No. 1, 2000, pp. 1–18.

Kols, Adrienne J., and Jill E. Sherman, "Family Planning Programs: Improving Quality," *Population Reports*, Series J, No. 47, Baltimore, Md.: Johns Hopkins University School of Public Health, Population Information Program, 1998.

Labbok, Miriam H., Virginia Hight-Laukaran, Anne E. Peterson, Veronica Fletcher, Helena von Hertzen, and Paul F. A. Van Look, "Multicenter Study of the Lactational Amenorrhea Method (LAM): I. Efficacy, Duration, and Implications for Clinical Application," *Contraception*, Vol. 55, 1997, pp. 327–336.

Lande, Robert E., "Controlling Sexually Transmitted Diseases," *Population Reports*, Series L, No. 9, 1993.

Lande, Robert E., and Judith S. Geller, "Paying for Family Planning," *Population Reports*, Series J, No. 39, Baltimore, Md.: Johns Hopkins University School of Public Health, Population Information Program, 1991.

Lapham, Robert J., and W. Parker Mauldin, "National Family Planning Programs: Review and Evaluation," *Studies in Family Planning*, Vol. 3, No. 3, 1972, pp. 29–52.

———, "Family Planning Program Effort and Birth Rate Decline in Developing Countries," *International Family Planning Perspectives*, Vol. 10, No. 4, 1984, p. 109–118.

———, "The Effects of Family Planning on Fertility: Research Findings," in Lapham, Robert, and George Simmons, eds., *Organizing for Effective Family Planning Programs*, Committee on Population, Washington, D.C.: National Academy Press, 1987.

Lapham, Robert, and George Simmons, eds., *Organizing for Effective Family Planning Programs*, Committee on Population, Washington, D.C.: National Academy Press, 1987.

Latin American and Caribbean Committee for the Defense of Women's Rights and the Center for Reproductive Law and Policy

(CRLP), *Silence and Complicity: Violence Against Women in Peruvian Public Health Facilities*, New York, 1999.

León, Federico R., "Introducing a Balanced Counseling Strategy with Interactive Job Aids: Effects on Provider's Quality of Care as Measured by the Service Test," *Peru PCI-QoC Project Bulletin*, No. 6, February 28, 2001, Population Council, Frontiers in Reproductive Health, 2001.

León, Federico R., Gustavo Quiroz, and Alfredo Brazzoduro, "The Reliability of Simulated Clients' Quality-of-Care Ratings," *Studies in Family Planning*, Vol. 25, No. 3, 1994, pp. 184–190.

Lorimer, Frank, *Culture and Fertility*, Paris: UNESCO, 1954.

Macro International, Inc., Demographic and Health Surveys, MEASURE DHS+, Publications Catalog, 1999a.

Maguire, Elizabeth S., "Meeting the Challenges: New Program Priorities and Initiatives for the Office of Population," U.S. Agency for International Development, paper presented at the Working Group on Reproductive Health and Family Planning of the Health and Development Policy Project, New York, May 1994.

Mahran, Maher, Fatma H. El-Zanaty, and Ann A. Way, *Perspectives on the Population and Health Situation in Egypt: Results of Further Analysis of the 1995 Egypt Demographic and Health Survey*, National Population Council, Cairo, Egypt, and Macro International, Inc., Calverton, Md., 1998.

Maine, Deborah, *Family Planning: Its Impact on the Health of Women and Children*, New York: The Center for Population and Family Health, Columbia University, 1981.

Mason, Karen Oppenheim, "Population Programs and Human Rights," in Ahlburg, Dennis A., Allen C. Kelley, and Karen Oppenheim Mason, eds., *The Impact of Population Growth on Well-Being in Developing Countries*, New York: Springer-Verlag, 1996, pp. 337–360.

Mauldin, W. Parker, and John A. Ross, "Family Planning Programs: Efforts and Results, 1982–1989," *Studies in Family Planning*, Vol. 22, No. 6, 1991, pp. 350–367.

McCauley, Ann P., and Judith S. Geller, "Decisions for Norplant Programs," *Population Reports*, Series K, No. 4, Baltimore, Md.: Johns Hopkins University, School of Public Health, Population Information Program, 1992.

McCauley, Ann P., and Cynthia Salter with Karungari Kiragu and Judith Senderowitz, "Meeting the Needs of Young Adults," *Population Reports*, Series J, No. 41, Baltimore, Md.: Johns Hopkins University, School of Public Health, Population Information Program, 1995.

McIntosh, C. Alison, and Jason L. Finkle, "The Cairo Conference on Population and Development," *Population and Development Review*, Vol. 21, No. 2, 1995, pp. 223–260.

McNicoll, Geoffrey, "The Governance of Fertility Transition: Reflections on the Asian Experience," in Jones, Gavin W., et al., *The Continuing Demographic Transition*, Oxford: Clarendon Press, 1997.

Mensch, Barbara, Andrew Fisher, Ian Askew, and Ayorinde Ajayi, "Using Situation Analysis Data to Assess the Functioning of Family Planning Clinics in Nigeria, Tanzania, and Zimbabwe," *Studies in Family Planning*, Vol. 25, No. 1, 1994, pp. 18–31.

Merrick, Thomas, personal electronic mail communication, Washington, D.C.: World Bank, February 11, 2000a.

——, personal electronic mail communication, Washington, D.C.: World Bank, October 13, 2000b.

Miller, Robert, Andrew Fisher, Kate Miller, Lewis Ndhlovu, Baker Ndugga Maggwa, Ian Askew, Diouratie Sanogo, and Placide Tapsoba, *The Situation Analysis Approach to Assessing Family Planning and Reproductive Health Services: A Handbook*, African Operations Research and Technical Assistance Project, Population Council, 1997.

Mirembe, Florence, Freddie Ssengooba, and Rosalind Lubanga, *Reproductive Health in Policy and Practice: Uganda*, Washington, D.C.: Population Reference Bureau, 1998.

Morris, Leo, Gary Lewis, D. L. Powell, J. Anderson, Ann Way, J. Cushing, and G. Lawless, "Contraceptive Prevalence Surveys: A

New Source of Family Planning Data," *Population Reports,* Series M., No. 5, Baltimore, Md.: The Johns Hopkins University, 1981.

Morris, Leo, "History and Current Status of Reproductive Health Surveys at CDC," *American Journal of Preventive Medicine,* Vol. 19, No. 1S, 2000, pp. 31–34.

Mosher, William D., Linda B. Williams, and David P. Johnson, "Religion and Fertility in the United States: New Patterns," *Demography,* Vol. 29, No. 2, 1992, pp. 199–214.

Mundigo, Axel I., "The Role of Family Planning Programmes in the Fertility Transition of Latin America," in Guzmán, José M., et al., *The Fertility Transition in Latin America,* Oxford: Clarendon Press, 1996.

Mundigo, Axel I., and Cynthia Indriso, eds., *Abortion in the Developing World,* London: World Health Organization, 1999.

Narayana, Gadde, J. S. Deepak, D. K. Mangal, K. M. Sathyanarayana, Ashok Kumar Singh, and Emily Pierce, *Making Things Happen: Decentralized Planning for RCH (Reproductive and Child Health) in Uttar Pradesh, India,* The Policy Project, New Delhi: The Futures Group International, 1999.

Narayana, Gadde, and A. Kameswara Rao, "Community Needs Assessment Approach in Andhra Pradesh," The Policy Project, New Delhi: The Futures Group International, draft paper, 1999.

Narvekar, Sharad, A. D. Pendse, and K. M. Sathyanarayana, "The Community Needs Assessment Approach for Family Welfare in Maharashtra," The Policy Project, New Delhi: The Futures Group International, draft paper, 2000.

National Academy of Sciences (NAS), *Population Growth and Economic Development: Policy Questions,* Committee on Population, National Research Council, Washington, D.C.: National Academy Press, 1986.

———, *Contraception and Reproduction: Health Consequences for Women and Children in the Developing World,* Committee on Population, National Research Council, Washington, D.C.: National Academy Press, 1989.

Nazzar, Alex, Philip B. Adongo, Fred N. Binka, James F. Phillips, and Cornelius Debpuur, "Developing a Culturally Appropriate Family Planning Program for the Navrongo Experiment," *Studies in Family Planning*, Vol. 26, No. 6, 1995, pp. 307–324.

Newman, Karen, personal electronic mail communication, London: IPPF, August 2, 2000a.

———, personal electronic mail communication, London: IPPF, September 26, 2000b.

———, personal electronic mail communications, London: IPPF, June 11 and June 19, 2001.

Nichiporuk, Brian, *The Security Dynamics of Demographic Factors*, Santa Monica, Calif.: RAND, 2000.

Noonan, John T., *Contraception: A History of Its Treatment by the Catholic Theologians and Canonists*, Cambridge, Mass.: Harvard University Press, 1986.

Nortman, Dorothy, and Ellen Hofstatter, "Population and Family Planning Programs: A Compendium on Data Through 1978," *A Population Council Factbook*, 1980.

Obermeyer, Carla Makhlouf, "Reproductive Choice in Islam: Gender and State in Iran and Tunisia," *Studies in Family Planning*, Vol. 25, No. 1, 1994, pp. 41–51.

Ortayli, Nuriye, Aysen Bulut, Hacer Nalbant, and Jane Cottingham, "Is the Diaphragm a Viable Options for Women in Turkey?" *International Family Planning Perspectives*, Vol. 26, No. 1, 2000, pp. 36–42.

ORC Macro, *DHS+ Dimensions*, Vol. 3, No. 1, 2001.

Pariani, Siti, David M. Heer, and Maurice D. Van Arsdol, Jr., "Does Choice Make a Difference to Contraceptive Use? Evidence from East Java," *Studies in Family Planning*, Vol. 22, No. 6, 1991, pp. 384–390.

Pathfinder International, "Family Planning and the Prevention of Abortion," Evaluation Unit and Public Affairs Department, 1999.

Phillips, James F., Ruth Simmons, Michael A. Koenig, and J. Chakraborty, "Determinants of Reproductive Change in a Traditional Society: Evidence from Matlab, Bangladesh," *Studies in Family Planning*, Vol. 19, No. 6/Part 1, 1988, pp. 313–334.

Phillips, James F., and John A. Ross, *Family Planning Programmes and Fertility*, Oxford: Clarendon Press, 1992.

Phillips, James F., Mian Bazle Hossain, and Mary Arends-Kuenning, "The Long-Term Demographic Role of Community-Based Family Planning in Rural Bangladesh," *Studies in Family Planning*, Vol. 27, No. 4, 1996, pp. 204–219.

Phillips, James F., Fred N. Binka, Martin Adjuik, Alex Nazzar, and Kubaje Adazu, "The Determinants of Contraceptive Innovation: A Case-Control Study of Family Planning Acceptance in a Traditional African Society," *Working Papers*, Policy Research Division, Population Council, No. 93, 1997.

Phillips, James F., and Mian Bazle Hossain, "The Impact of Family Planning Household Service Delivery on Women's Status in Bangladesh," *Working Papers*, Policy Research Division, Population Council, No. 118, 1998.

Pile, John M., Cidem Bumin, Arzum Cilolu, and Aye Akin, "Involving Men as Partners in Reproductive Health: Lessons from Turkey," *AVSC Working Paper*, AVSC International, No. 12, 1999.

Pillsbury, Barbara, Francine Coeytaux, and Andrea Johnston, *From Secret to Shelf: How Collaboration Is Bringing Emergency Contraception to Women*, Los Angeles, Calif.: Pacific Institute for Women's Health in Collaboration with the David and Lucile Packard Foundation, 1999.

Population Action International, *Washington Population Update: New Analysis of U.S. and International Population Assistance*, Washington, D.C., June 2000.

Population Council, *Operations Research Summaries, Operations Research and Technical Assistance—Improving Family Planning and Reproductive Health Services Worldwide*, New York, 1998a.

————, *Reproductive Health Operations Research, 1995–1998*, INOPAL III, Mexico City, 1998b.

————, "Frontiers in Reproductive Health Electronic Library 1990–1999," Washington, D.C., 2000.

Population Reference Bureau, Inc. (PRB), *Family Planning Saves Lives: A Strategy for Maternal and Child Survival*, Washington, D.C.: The IMPACT Project, 1986.

————, World Population Data Sheet 2001, Washington, D.C., 2001.

Potter, Joseph E., "The Persistence of Outmoded Contraceptive Regimes," *Population and Development Review*, Vol. 25, No. 4, 1999, pp. 703–739.

Pritchett, Lant H., "Desired Fertility and the Impact of Population Policies," *Population and Development Review*, Vol. 20, No. 1, 1994, pp. 1–55.

Program for Appropriate Technology in Health (PATH), "Men and Reproductive Health," *Reproductive Health Outlook*, Washington, D.C.: www.rho.org/html/menrh.htm (as of November 2001), 2001.

Raghunath, Rajiv, "Dividends of a Participatory Plan," *The Financial Express*, New Delhi, August 8, 1999.

Rahman, Mizanur, Julie DaVanzo, and Abdur Razzaque, "Do Better Family Planning Services Reduce Abortion in Bangladesh?" *The Lancet*, Vol. 358, No. 9287, 2001, pp. 1051–1056.

Reddy, Ramakrishna, P. Hanumantharayappa, and K. M. Sathyanarayana, "The Community Needs Assessment Approach in Karnataka, The POLICY Project, New Delhi: The Futures Group International, draft paper, 2000.

Reich, Warren Thomas, editor-in-chief, *Encyclopedia of Bioethics*, revised ed., New York: Simon & Schuster Macmillan, 1995.

Rinehart, Ward, and Adrienne Kols with Sidney H. Moore, "Healthier Mothers and Children Through Family Planning," *Population Reports*, Series J, No. 27, Baltimore, Md.: Johns Hopkins School of Public Health, Population Information Program, 1984.

Robey, Bryant, Shea O. Rutstein, and Leo Morris with Richard Blackburn, "The Reproductive Revolution: New Survey Findings," *Population Reports*, Series M, No. 11, Baltimore, Md.: Johns Hopkins School of Public Health, Population Information Program, 1992.

Robey, Bryant, Phyllis T. Piotrow, and Cynthia Salter, "Family Planning Lessons and Challenges: Making Programs Work," *Population Reports*, Series J, No. 40, Baltimore, Md.: Johns Hopkins School of Public Health, Population Information Program, 1994.

Romero, Hernan, "Chile: The Abortion Epidemic," in Berelson, Bernard, ed., *Family Planning Programs: An International Survey*, New York: Basic Books, Inc., 1969.

Rosero-Bixby, Luis, personal electronic mail communication, San José: University of Costa Rica, June 27, 2001.

Ross, John A., and Rodolfo A. Bulatao, "Contraceptive Projections and the Donor Gap," Washington, D.C.: The Futures Group International for John Snow, Inc., Family Planning Logistics Management Project, 2001.

Ross, John, Donald J. Lauro, Joe D. Wray, and Allan G. Rosenfield, "Community-based Distribution," in Lapham, Robert, and George Simmons, eds., *Organizing for Effective Family Planning Programs*, Committee on Population, Washington, D.C.: National Academy Press, 1987.

Ross, John A. and Cynthia Lloyd, "Methods for Measuring the Fertility Impact of Family Planning Programs: The Experience of the Last Decade, " in Phillips, James F., and John A. Ross, *Family Planning Programmes and Fertility*, Oxford: Clarendon Press, 1992.

Ross, John A., and W. Parker Mauldin, "Family Planning Programs: Efforts and Results, 1972–94, *Studies in Family Planning*, Vol. 27, No. 3, 1996, pp. 137–147.

Ross, John, John Stover, and Amy Willard, *Profiles for Family Planning and Reproductive Health Programs, 116 Countries*, Glastonbury, Conn.: The Futures Group International, 1999.

Routh, Subrata, Ali Ashraf, John Stoeckel, and Barkat-e-Khuda, "Consequences of the Shift from Domiciliary Distribution to Site-Based Family Planning Services in Bangladesh," *International Family Planning Perspectives,* Vol. 27, No. 2, 2001, pp. 82–89.

Sadik, Nafis, "United Nations Population Fund (UNFPA)," in Wallace, Helen M., and Giri Kanti, *Health Care of Women and Children in Developing Countries,* Oakland, Calif.: Third Party Publishing Company, 1990.

Salter, Cynthia, Heidi Bart Johnston, and Nicolene Hengren, "Care for Postabortion Complications: Saving Women's Lives," *Population Reports,* Series L, No. 10, Baltimore, Md.: Johns Hopkins University, School of Public Health, Population Information Program, 1997.

Samara, Renee, Bates Buckner, and Amy Ong Tsui, *Understanding How Family Planning Programs Work: Findings from Five Years of Evaluation Research,* Chapel Hill, N.C.: The EVALUATION Project, Carolina Population Center, University of North Carolina, 1996.

Schuler, Sidney, "Gender and Community Participation in Reproductive Health Projects: Contrasting Models from Peru and Ghana," John Snow, Inc. Research and Training Institute, 1999.

Schuler, Sidney Ruth, Syed M. Hashemi, Amy Cullum, and Mirza Hassan, "The Advent of Family Planning as a Social Norm in Bangladesh: Women's Experiences," *Reproductive Health Matters,* No. 7, 1996, pp. 66–78.

Schuler, Sidney Ruth, and Zakir Hossain, "Family Planning Clinics Through Women's Eyes and Voices: A Case Study from Rural Bangladesh," *International Family Planning Perspectives,* Vol. 24, No. 4, 1998, pp. 170–175.

Seltzer, Judith R., Karen Johnson Lassner, and S. Ken Yamashita, *Mid-term Program Review of the U.S.–Mexico Program of Collaboration on Population and Reproductive Health,* POPTECH Report No. 96-083-049, 1997.

Seltzer, Judith R., and Fernando Gomez, *Family Planning and Population Programs in Colombia: 1965–1997,* POPTECH Report No. 97-114-062, 1998.

Senderowitz, Judith, "Making Reproductive Health Services Youth Friendly," FOCUS on Young Adults Project, Pathfinder International, 1999.

Shane, Barbara, and Kate Chalkley, *From Research to Action: How Operations Research Is Improving Reproductive Health Services*, Washington, D.C.: Population Reference Bureau, 1998.

Sharma, O. P., "India Proposes Retooled Population Policy," *Population Today*, Washington, D.C.: Population Reference Bureau, Vol. 28, No. 3, 2000.

Shelton, James D., "The Provider Perspective: Human After All," *International Family Planning Perspectives*, Vol. 27, No. 3, 2001, pp. 152–161.

————, Sarah Davis, and Jill Mathis, "Maximizing Access and Quality: Checklist for Family Planning Service Delivery, with Selected Linkages to Reproductive Health," Office of Population, U.S. Agency for International Development, Version 1.1, 1998.

Sheon, Amy, William Schellstede, and Bonnie Derr, "Contraceptive Social Marketing," in Lapham, Robert, and George Simmons, eds., *Organizing for Effective Family Planning Programs*, Committee on Population, Washington, D.C.: National Academy Press, 1987, pp. 367–390.

Simmons, George, "Demand and Supply, Not Supply vs. Demand: Appropriate Theory for the Study of Effects of Family Planning Programmes on Fertility," in Phillips, James F., and John A. Ross, *Family Planning Programmes and Fertility*, Oxford: Clarendon Press, 1992.

Simmons, Ruth, Review of "The Evolving Rationale for Family Planning Programs," August 31, 2000, electronic mail communication to RAND, September 2000.

Simmons, Ruth, and George B. Simmons, "The Task Environment of Family Planning" in Lapham, Robert, and George Simmons, eds., *Organizing for Effective Family Planning Programs*, Committee on Population, Washington, D.C.: National Academy Press, 1987.

Simmons, Ruth, and James E. Phillips, "The Integration of Family Planning with Health and Development," in Lapham, Robert, and George Simmons, eds., *Organizing for Effective Family Planning Programs*, Committee on Population, Washington, D.C.: National Academy Press, 1987.

Simmons, Ruth, Rezina Mita, and Michael A. Koenig, "Employment in Family Planning and Women's Status in Bangladesh," *Studies in Family Planning*, Vol. 23, No. 2, 1992, pp. 97–109.

Simmons, Ruth, and Christopher Elias, "The Study of Client–Provider Interactions: A Review of Methodological Issues," *Studies in Family Planning*, Vol. 25, No. 1, 1994, pp. 1–17.

Simmons, Ruth, and Anne M. Young, *Family Planning Programs and Other Interventions to Assist Women: Their Impact on Demographic Change and on the Status of Women*, Honolulu: Program on Population, East–West Center, 1996.

Simmons, Ruth, Peter Hall, Juan Díaz, Margarita Díaz, Peter Fajans, and Jay Satia, "The Strategic Approach to Contraceptive Introduction," *Studies in Family Planning*, Vol. 28, No. 2, 1997, pp. 79–94.

Simon, Julian, *The Ultimate Resource*, Princeton, N.J.: Princeton University Press, 1981.

Sinding, Steven W., "The Great Population Debates: How Relevant for the 21st Century?" *American Journal of Public Health*, Vol. 90, No. 12, 2001, pp. 1841–1847.

Sinding, Steven W., John A. Ross, and Allan G. Rosenfield, "Seeking Common Ground: Unmet Need and Demographic Goals," *International Family Planning Perspectives*, Vol. 20, No. 1, 1994, pp. 23–32.

Singh, Susheela, Deidre Wulf, Renee Samara, and Yvette P. Cuca, "Gender Differences in the Timing of First Intercourse: Data for 14 Countries," *International Family Planning Perspectives*, Vol. 26, No. 1, 2000, pp. 21–28.

Smyth, Ines, "The Indonesian Family Planning Programme: A Success Story for Women?" *Development and Change*, Vol. 22, 1991, pp. 781–805.

Sociedad Civil Bem-Estar Familiar no Brasil, *Pesquisa Nacional Sobre Saude Materno-Infantil Planejamento Familiar: Brasil 1986*, Rio de Janeiro: BEMFAM, 1986.

Speidel, J. Joseph, personal communication, Menlo Park, Calif.: Hewlitt Foundation, September 4, 2000.

Speizer, Ilene, David R. Hotchkiss, Robert J. Magnani, Brian Hubbard, and Kristen Nelson, "Do Service Providers in Tanzania Unnecessarily Restrict Clients' Access to Contraceptive Methods?" *International Family Planning Perspectives*, Vol. 26, No. 1, 2000, pp. 13–20.

Spicehandler, Joanne, and Ruth Simmons, *Contraceptive Introduction Reconsidered: A Review and Conceptual Framework*, Special Programme of Research, Development, and Research Training in Human Reproduction, Geneva: World Health Organization, 1994.

Stash, Sharon, "Explanation of Unmet Need for Contraception in Chitwan, Nepal," *Studies in Family Planning*, Vol. 30, No. 4, 1999, pp. 267–287.

Tan Boon Ann, "Multivariate Areal Analysis of the Impact and Efficiency of the Family Planning Programme in Peninsular Malaysia," *Asia-Pacific Population Journal*, Vol. 2, No. 2, 1987, pp. 45–66.

Terborgh, Anne, James E. Rosen, Roberto Saniso Galvez, Willy Terceros, Jane T. Bertrand, and Sheana E. Bull, "Family Planning Among Indigenous Populations in Latin America," *International Family Planning Perspectives*, Vol. 21, No. 4, 1995, pp. 143–149.

Timmer, Peter C., Ismail Sirageldin, John Kantner, and Samuel H. Preston, Review Symposium on Julian L. Simon's *The Ultimate Resource, Population and Development Review*, Vol. 8, No. 1, 1982, pp. 163–177.

Tsui, Amy O., Judith N. Wasserheit, and John G. Haaga, eds., *Reproductive Health in Developing Countries: Expanding Dimensions, Building Solutions*, Washington, D.C.: National Academy Press, 1997.

United Nations (UN), "World Population Plan of Action," in *Population and Development Review*, Vol. 1, No. 1, 1975, pp. 163–181.

———, *Population Policies and Programmes: Proceedings of the United Nations Expert Group Meeting on Population Policies and Programmes*, Cairo, Egypt, Department of Economic and Social Affairs, Population Division, New York: United Nations, 1993.

———, Program of Action of the 1994 International Conference on Population and Development (Chapters I–VIII), in *Population and Development Review*, Vol. 21, No. 1, 1995, pp. 187–213.

———, "UNFPA Mission Statement and a Common Advocacy Statement on Population and Development by the United Nations System," reproduced in Documents, *Population and Development Review*, Vol. 22, No. 3, 1996, pp. 595–600.

———, *National Population Policies*, Department of Economic and Social Affairs, Population Division, New York: United Nations, 1998.

———, *Levels and Trends of Contraceptive Use as Assessed in 1998*, Department of Economic and Social Affairs, Population Division, New York: United Nations, 1999a.

———, excerpt from The Global Report on the HIV/AIDS Epidemic in *Population and Development Review*, Vol. 26, No. 3, 2000a, pp. 629–633.

———, *Global Population Database, 1999*, Department of Economic and Social Affairs, Population Division, New York: United Nations, 2000b.

———, *World Population Prospects: The 2000 Revision*, Department of Economic and Social Affairs, Population Division, New York: United Nations, 2001.

United Nations Population Fund (UNFPA), *The State of World Population 1997*, "The Right to Choose: Reproductive Rights and Reproductive Health," New York: UNFPA, 1997.

———, *The State of World Population 1999*, "6 Billion: A Time for Choices," New York: UNFPA, 1999a.

————, *Global Population Assistance Report 1997*, New York: UNFPA, 1999b.

————, *The State of World Population 2000*, "Lives Together, World Apart: Men and Women in a Time of Change," New York: UNFPA, 2000a.

————, *Financial Resource Flows for Population Activities in 1998*, New York: UNFPA, 2000b.

U.S. Agency for International Development (USAID), *A.I.D. Policy Paper: Population Assistance*, Bureau for Program and Policy Coordination, Washington, D.C.: September 1982.

————, Bureau for Latin America and the Caribbean, "Surgical Contraception in the Government of Peru Family Planning Program: A Report from the Field," Washington, D.C., 1999a.

————, "Guidance for Implementing the 'Tiahrt' Requirements for Voluntary Family Planning Projects," Washington, D.C., 1999b.

————, "Users' Guide to USAID/Washington Population, Health and Nutrition Programs," Center for Population, Health, and Nutrition, Washington, D.C., 2000.

USAID/Mexico, facsimile with the definition of *demanda calificada* (informed demand) developed by the National Population Council in Mexico, Mexico City, 2000.

USAID/Peru, "Two Years on the Ground: ReproSalud Through Women's Eyes," Lima, 1999.

U.S. Bureau of the Census, *International Brief, World Population at a Glance: 1998 and Beyond*, Washington, D.C.: U.S. Government Printing Office, 1999.

Vaessen, Martin, "Survey Costs," facsimile communication from Macro International, Inc., Calverton, Md., July 18, 2000.

Varga, Christine A., "South African Young People's Sexual Dynamics: Implications for Behavioral Reponses to HIV/AIDS," *Resistances to Behavioural Change to Reduce HIV/AIDS Infection in Predominantly Heterosexual Epidemics in Third World Countries,*

Canberra, Australia: Health Transition Centre, Australian National University, 1999.

Vera, Hernan, "The Client's View of High-Quality Care in Santiago, Chile," *Studies in Family Planning*, Vol. 24, No. 1, 1993, pp. 40–49.

Visaria, Pravin, and Vijaylaxmi Chari, "India's Population Policy and Family Planning Program: Yesterday, Today, and Tomorrow," in Jain, Anrudh, ed., *Do Population Policies Matter? Fertility and Politics in Egypt, India, Kenya, and Mexico,* New York: The Population Council, 1998.

Visaria, Leela, Shireen Jejeebhoy, and Tom Merrick, "From Family Planning to Reproductive Health: Challenges Facing India," *International Family Planning Perspectives*, Vol. 25 (Suppl.), 1999, pp. S44–S49.

Warwick, Donald P., *Bitter Pills: Population Policies and Their Implementation in Eight Developing Countries,* New York: Cambridge University Press, 1982.

———, "The Indonesian Family Planning Program: Government Influence and Client Choice," *Population and Development Review*, Vol. 12, No. 3, 1986, pp. 453–490.

Wattenberg, Ben, "Miscast Fertility Forecasts," *The Washington Times,* March 8, 2001, p. A16.

Westoff, Charles F., "The Unmet Need for Birth Control in Five Asian Countries," *International Family Planning Perspective and Digest,* Vol. 4, No. 1, 1978, pp. 9–18.

———, "Reproductive Intentions and Fertility Rates," *International Family Planning Perspectives*, Vol. 16, No. 3, 1990, pp. 84–96.

Westoff, Charles F., and Akinrinola Bankole, "Trends in the Demand for Family Limitation in Developing Countries," *International Family Planning Perspectives*, Vol. 26, No. 2, 2000, pp. 56–62.

Westoff, Charles F., Almaz Sharmanov, Jeremiah P. Sullivan, and Trevor Croft, *The Replacement of Abortion by Contraception in Three Central Asian Republics,* Calverton, MD: The Policy Project and Macro International, Inc., 1998.

Williams, Timothy, Jessie Schutt-Aine, and Yvette Cuca, "Measuring Family Planning Service Quality Through Client Satisfaction Exit Interviews," *International Family Planning Perspectives*, Vol. 26, No. 2, 2000, pp. 63–71.

Winikoff, Beverly, and Maureen Sullivan, "Assessing the Role of Family Planning in Reducing Maternal Mortality," *Studies in Family Planning*, Vol. 18, No. 3, 1987, pp. 128–143.

Women's Environment and Development Organization (WEDO), *Risks, Rights and Reforms: A 50-Country Survey Assessing Government Actions Five Years After the International Conference on Population and Development*, New York, 1999.

World Bank, *Population and the World Bank: Adapting to Change*, The Human Development Network: Health, Nutrition, and Population Series, Washington, D.C., 2000.

World Health Organization (WHO), *Creating Common Ground: Women's Perspective on the Selection and Introduction of Fertility Regulation Technologies*, WHO/HRP/ITT, Geneva: WHO, 1991.

———, *Improving Access to Quality Care in Family Planning: Medical Eligibility Criteria for Initiating and Continuing Use of Contraceptive Methods*, Geneva: WHO, 1996.

Yinger, Nancy, *Unmet Need for Family Planning: Reflecting Women's Perceptions*, Washington, D.C.: International Center for Research on Women, 1998.

n = note.